BRITISH COLUMBIA:
A WALKING GUIDE

About the Author

In 1996 Janna Leigh Fleming left the Univeristy of British Columbia with a degree in geography, a passion for travel and a love of research, oceans, islands and coasts. After beginning a major in anthropology, she realised it was not just people and cultures that deeply affected her, but also the land and the sea, the tides changing with the moon, the rising of the sun, the growth of a tree and the hidden lives of animals. She has spent five years living and roaming around Hawaii, southwest England and her hometown in Nova Scotia. Currently she has found an inspiring sense of quiet and calm in Haida Gwaii, British Columbia, amidst the eagles, ravens, wind-swept beaches and rocky shores. She finds immense satisfaction in writing about the people and places that have found a way inside her soul. Having accepted that restlessness and a desire to seek new pastures is not a passing phase (or a personality flaw), she strives to divide her time between the people and places she calls home and the unknown spaces in the world which draw her with the promise of something new. Janna Leigh Fleming is a freelance writer and news editor for *Big World* magazine, an American publication aimed at the independent traveller. This is her first book.

BRITISH COLUMBIA:

A WALKING GUIDE

by

Janna Leigh Fleming

CICERONE PRESS
MILNTHORPE, CUMBRIA LA7 7PY
www.cicerone.co.uk

© Janna Leigh Fleming 2002

ISBN 1 85284 340 3

Maps and photos (unless otherwise credited) are by Janna Leigh Fleming. Photographs from the pole-raising ceremonies of June 2001 at Qay'llnagaay are used with the permission of the Qay'llnagaay Heritage Centre Society. Other photos are by Martijn Coini and Jonathan Deakin. Sketches by Jason Thibault.

A catalogue record for this book is available from the British Library.

Acknowledgements

Many people have helped me in the research and preparation of this guidebook. Others have simply been an endless source of inspiration and encouragement. In particular I would like to thank Lana Cheong from Tourism BC; BC Ferries; Laidlaw Coachlines; all the helpful staff at Parks Canada, BC Parks, and the Visitors' Centres; Martijn Coini and Jonathan Deakin for their slides; Adrienne Hennessey for getting her feet cold, wet and muddy in the early days and for giving me a home in the later ones; Janet Seney for her sofa and drives to/from the airport in Vancouver; all the guys at Urban Surfer in Exeter for the extensive time off and for their support; Jason Thibault for his amazing drawings; Steve for his encouragement; Jonathan Williams and the team at Cicerone for their input; Carolyn and Cacilia in Haida Gwaii for their kindness; all my family and friends especially my mum; and for Andy who made me see that heaven is right here. Thank you all.

ADVICE TO READERS

Readers are advised that while every effort is taken by the author to ensure the accuracy of this guidebook, changes can occur which may affect the contents. It is advisable to check locally on transport, accommodation, shops, etc, but even rights of way can be altered.

The publisher would welcome notes of any such changes.

Front cover: *Yoho National Park*

CONTENTS

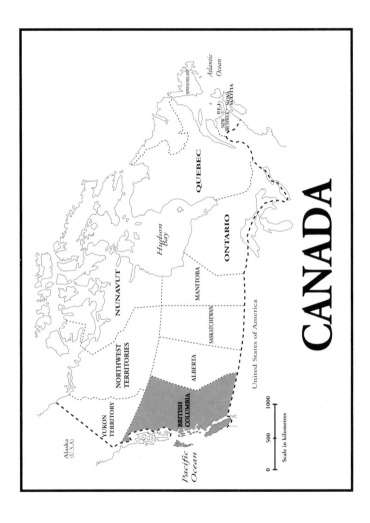

FOREWORD

The walks in this book are meant to inspire. With a balance between coast and mountains, they offer a glimpse, or a taste, of what British Columbia has to offer. Some of the walks are easy and short, others are strenuous and may lead for days through ice-capped peaks or along endless wind-swept beaches. All are significant in that they bring us to a world we are often so far removed from. Besides the wilderness, it is the cultures of the First Nations people that draw visitors to BC, and there are many areas of cultural significance: areas with rock drawings, ancient burial sites, weathering totem poles and abandoned villages. The First Nations cultures in BC are thriving and very much alive today. The introductory sections and some of the trail descriptions touch on some of the First Nations groups (see also Appendix B) that live in the areas, and their histories and legends. These are merely an introduction, and do not aim to speak for any of these nations, for their voices are loud and they can and do speak for themselves. These sections are included because their histories go back thousands and thousands of years, and the people have maintained such strong ties to the land, the environment and nature.

The book is a great mixture of long and short walks both easy and difficult. The longer trails require the hiker to be self-sufficient and camp along the route. It is very important that hikers be aware of their abilities. Most hikes offer alternative routes for those looking for an extra challenge or for an easier route out. And this is but a glimpse; there are more areas than just these, some hidden, some right there in front of you.

Open your eyes and ears to a wonderful place. I invite you to walk with me.

Janna Leigh Fleming

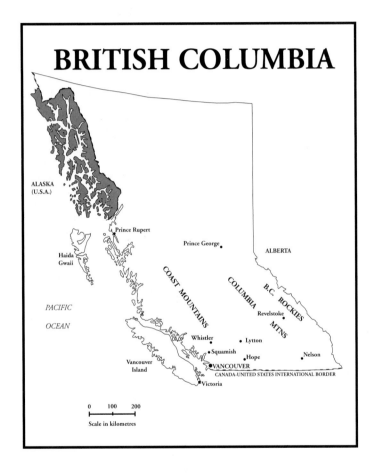

BRITISH COLUMBIA

ALASKA
(U.S.A.)

• Prince Rupert

Haida
Gwaii

Prince George •

ALBERTA

COAST MOUNTAINS

COLUMBIA

B.C. ROCKIES

PACIFIC

OCEAN

MTNS

Revelstoke •

Whistler •

• Lytton

• Squamish

• Hope

• Nelson

Vancouver
Island

●VANCOUVER

CANADA–UNITED STATES INTERNATIONAL BORDER

•Victoria

```
0      100    200
├───┼───┤
Scale in kilometres
```

INTRODUCTION

British Columbia is probably best known for its trees, its fish, its mountains, its islands and the city of Vancouver. Visitors flock to the area from all over the world; eastern Canadians feel a strange magnetic pull westward; and immigrants from everywhere come here to begin a new life in this amazing place. The Canadian wilderness is beautiful, sacred. Some places are remote beyond belief with a supreme sense of solitude; others are jubilantly busy with people enjoying themselves and their environment. The Canadian wilderness gives the very meaning to the words pristine and rugged and immediately fills us with feelings of awe, wonder and reverence. And there's something very special about the west coast of Canada; its inhabitants know it, respect it and fight to keep it. The majesty of the Rockies humbles us, the Pacific Ocean constantly reminds us of our fragility and powerlessness, the vast biodiversity weaves its web around us and the strength of the First Nations peoples – with their cultures, traditions and perpetual ties to the land – enthralls us.

British Columbia (or BC as it is called by Canadians) is Canada's gateway to the Pacific. Isolated from the rest of Canada by the snow-capped, awe-inspiring peaks of the Rocky Mountains, it remains uniquely distinctive both geographically and culturally. From the tops of the mountains to the crashing waves of the Pacific Ocean, from the coastal rainforests to the interior plateauxs, from the subalpine meadows and glacial lakes to the freshwater rivers, BC offers the hiker more than 3000km of trails within its provincial parks alone and more than 11.5 million hectares of protected land. As the westernmost province of Canada, BC borders Alberta to the east; the Yukon and Northwest Territories to the north; the Pacific Ocean to the west; the American states of Washington and Montana to the south; and the Alaska to the northwest. BC is four times the size of the UK and bigger than every American state except for Alaska. It is Canada's third largest province, and with a land and freshwater area of 95 million hectares BC makes up 9.5% of the total landmass of the country.

For the outdoor enthusiast, BC is paradise. It is home to Canada's greatest diversity of plants and animals (including many protected species): from sockeye salmon runs to killer whale pods to gigantic red cedar trees to grizzly bears or seabirds. There are 637 provincial parks, recreation areas and ecological reserves, and six national parks to explore. BC has the country's second largest parks system, after Canada's national parks. In 1992, BC adopted the Protected Areas Strategy that 'reflects the commitment to a balance between significant environmental protection, sustainable economic development and community stability'. Since 1991, BC has doubled its number of parks and protected areas. Protected areas include land, freshwater and marine areas, and these are set aside as nature preserves, research and educational areas or for recreational use.

BC's habitats support a great diversity of plants and animals, including 454 species of birds, 143 land mammals, 20 amphibians, 19 reptiles and 450 fish species. These make up more than 50% of Canada's wildlife species. As well, BC has 15,000 plant species, of which 600 are considered rare, vulnerable or endangered. BC contains 75% of the world's stone sheep, 60% of its mountain goats, 50% of its blue grouse, 50% of its trumpeter swans and 25% of its grizzly bears and bald eagles. Of BC's 5 million nesting seabirds, 70% are protected in ecological reserves.

The human population of British Columbia is about 3.5 million, with the majority living in cosmopolitan Vancouver. But even in the hustle and bustle of the metropolis, the people in Vancouver remain laid-back and friendly. With the Coast Mountains providing the backdrop and the Strait of Georgia the foreground, the mountains and the beaches play a vital role in the city-dwellers' everyday lives, a gigantic playground right in their backyard. Outside of Vancouver are smaller cities, bigger mountains and lots of islands. The wanderer could spend weeks, months, years or a lifetime soaking it all in – perhaps taking a break to ski in the Rockies, surf Long Beach on Vancouver Island or kayak Gwaii Haanas in Haida Gwaii.

GETTING THERE

Flights to Canada and British Columbia depart from every major airport in the UK. Most visitors fly to Vancouver, and either stay there for a while or catch a connecting flight out. Visitors to the BC Rockies may wish to fly into Calgary (Alberta) instead. Travellers with time to explore could fly into Vancouver and out of Calgary or vice versa.

Canadian Affair: www.canadian-affair.com Canadian Affair is a UK company specializing in Canadian flights. It has partnered with JMC Airlines and Air Tours International, and their website always has specials – tickets can be easily purchased online. Tel: (London) (020) 7616-9184, (Glasgow) (0141) 248-6777, (National) (0870) 753-000.

Air Canada/Canadian: www.aircanada.ca Air Canada is Canada's largest airline with international and domestic flights to hundreds of destinations, big or small. Visit the Star Alliance Ticket Office, 7/8 Conduit Street, London W1R 9TG, ring Air Canada (UK reservations) (08705) 247-226 (or 1-888-AIR-CANADA within Canada) or reserve a ticket online.

Air Transat: www.airtransat.com Online reservations, or tel. (within Canada) 1-866-847-1112

British Airways: www.britishairways.com Online reservations, or tel. (0845) 773-3377

KLM Royal Dutch Airlines: www.klmuk.co.uk For reservations call (08705) 074-074

Passports and Visas
Passports are required for every visitor wishing to enter Canada except citizens of the United States, who only require proof of citizenship and at least one photo ID. British, Australian and most European citizens do not need visas to enter the country – if unsure, check the list at www.canadiantourism.com or contact the Canadian embassy in your home country.

STAYING IN BRITISH COLUMBIA

Getting Around
Visitors wishing to drive should obtain an International Driving Permit from the Automobile Association (AA) in their home country. They are usually valid for up to a year. All American drivers licences are valid in Canada and vice versa. Canadians drive on the right-hand side of the road. Speed limits vary and are posted, but generally limits are 50km/hr in cities, 30km/hr in school zones or areas with lots of

The Lootaa – *a 50ft Haida cedar canoe*

children, and 60km/hr or 110km/hr on highways and in rural areas, depending on the location. The use of seatbelts is mandatory at all times, and adults are responsible for anyone under the age of 16 in the car and must ensure that they are belted in. British Columbia has strict anti-drinking and driving laws, and random road-checks are common in both cities and rural areas.

Traffic may be minimal outside urban areas and in sparsely populated northern BC. However, expect to find the national parks, and in particular the BC Rockies, extremely busy during the peak summer season.

Highways and roads are generally in good condition, and visitors will find them much wider than in the UK. Some access roads to the trails in this guide are side roads, gravel roads and logging roads (see 'Driving and Logging Roads' in 'On the Trail'). When driving in mountain areas and through passes, be prepared for all weather conditions: even on a late spring day drivers may find themselves in a snowstorm at high elevation!

Petrol stations and garages are scarce in northern BC and some rural areas, but are posted, so watch for road signs such as 'Last gas station for 100km'.

Car Rental

All the major car rental companies can be found in British Columbia – check in the airport or individual visitor centres in cities or towns. The two companies below are known for the best deals.

Alamo Car Rental-www.alamo.com Alamo only has offices in Calgary and Vancouver, but they offer superb rates and discounts on internet reservations. For travellers wishing to explore both the coast and the Rockies, one option is to rent a car in Vancouver and pay a small drop-off fee to return it in Calgary. It is often possible to fly into one and out of the other for no extra charge – because British Columbia is so big, this saves a lot of travelling time.

Rent-A-Wreck-www.rentawreck.ca Rent-A-Wreck has offices all over British Columbia and offers affordable rental rates by the day, week or month. For reservations, call 1-800-327-0116.

Buses and Passes

Greyhound Bus Lines: www.greyhound.ca

International Canada Coach Pass: choose 7 days' unlimited travel within: 10 days, 15 days in 20, 30 days in 40, or 60 days in 80. The pass must be purchased overseas. In the UK, call (01342) 317317 or fax (01342) 328519.

Domestic Canada Coach Pass: similar to the International pass except that it can be purchased in Canada but it must be purchased 7 days in advance.

Laidlaw/Grayline of Victoria: operates scheduled services to most communities on Vancouver Island. www.victoriatours.com

Pacific Coach Lines: a bus and ferry service between Vancouver and Victoria, tel. 1-800-661-1725

BC Transit: public transit schedules throughout the province (except Greater Vancouver). www.transitbc.com

Vancouver Airporter: most travellers will fly into Vancouver. This bus service connects the airport with several destinations in Vancouver. For schedules and times, call (604) 946-8866 or 1-800-668-3141.

Backpacker Buses

Moose Run Adventure Tours
1653 Coquitlam Avenue
Coquitlam, BC V3B 1H8
Tel. (604) 944-3007 or toll-free 1-888-388-4881
www.mooserun.com

The Moose Run is a hop-on-hop-off backpacker bus that does a 10-day circular route covering Vancouver–Whistler–Kamloops–Jasper–Lake Louise–Banff–Kelowna–Penticton–Manning Park–Vancouver. It stops off at Hostelling International hostels along the way and also offers short guided hikes and other activities. It is a fun and inexpensive way to travel around the province for those who either don't want to rent a car or are travelling alone and want to meet up with other like-minded travellers.

Bigfoot Adventure Tours
1900 Valmont Way
Richmond, BC V6V 1Y4
Tel. (604) 278-8224
Fax (604) 278-4881
www.bigfoottours.com

Bigfoot has the two-day Roadrunner Tour between Vancouver and Banff and a seven-day loop calling at Vancouver–Whistler–Kamloops–Jasper–Banff–Revelstoke–Kelowna–Vancouver.

Seagull Bus
tel. 1-800-580-3890
www.seagullbus.com

Seagull Bus has a five-day loop covering Vancouver–Victoria–Long Beach–Tofino–Vancouver.

Rail

VIA Rail is Canada's national passenger train service. Check out their website for destinations and schedules (www.viarail.ca). A CANRAIL Pass is valid anywhere VIA Rail goes and is valid for 12 days of unlimited travel within a 30-day period. A North America Rail Pass combines the services of VIA Rail in Canada and Amtrak in the

United States. It is valid for 30 days of unlimited travel on a 45,000km rail network that connects over 900 cities and communities in Canada and the US. Both passes can be booked in the UK from Leisurerail, PO Box 5, 12 Coningsby Road, Peterborough, PE3 8XP, www.leisurail.co.uk.

BC Rail operates passenger services between North Vancouver and Prince George and North Vancouver and Squamish and Whistler. The station is located at 1311 West First Street in North Vancouver. Check out www.bcrail.com for more information or call (604) 984-5246 or 1-800-339-8752 (in BC) or 1-800-663-8238 (outside BC).

Ferries
BC Ferries: www.bcferries.bc.ca The website has complete up-to-date information on schedules, ferries and reservations. Passenger service agents: tel. (250) 386-3431 outside BC or 1-888-BCFERRY inside BC. Vehicle reservations: tel. (604) 444-2890 outside BC or 1-888-724-5223 inside BC.

By Air
Besides all the major airlines already listed, here are a few other suggestions:
Hawkair: tel. (250) 635-4295 or 1-866-HAWKAIR (toll-free in Canada), www.hawkair.net; service between Vancouver and Terrace or Prince Rupert
Baxter Air: 22 daily flights between Nanaimo and Vancouver
Air BC: tel. (250) 360-9074 or 1-800-663-3721; Vancouver Island
Canadian Regional Airlines: tel. 1-800-665-1177; Vancouver Island
Helijet Airways: tel. (250) 382-6222 or 1-800-665-4354; between Vancouver, Victoria and Seattle
Harbour Air: tel. (250) 384-2215 or 1-800-665-0212; scheduled seaplane service between Vancouver and Victoria
West Jet: tel. 1-888-WESTJET or (403) 444-2552, www.westjet.com; flights to/from Vancouver, Victoria, Kelowna, Abbotsford, Prince George, Calgary and others.

Cycling
BC is a very cycle-friendly place with lots of bike paths. Just remember, bicycle helmets are mandatory in British Columbia.

Although many of the hiking trails in parks are closed to cycles, some parks have converted fire roads into great backcountry mountain-biking trails. Check at the local information centres for details on cycling trails in the area.

Accommodation
B&Bs, Hotels, Motels
BC Tourism produces an excellent free annual guide to help visitors choose the accommodation which best suits their desires and budgets. The guide covers all regions of British Columbia. Call 1-800-HELLOBC (453-5622) or check out www.HelloBC.com for your copy of the *Approved Accommodations Guide*. The above telephone number will also help you with reservations and other travel ideas.

Hostels
Hostelling International Canada
British Columbia Regional Office
Suite #402, 134 Abbott Street
Vancouver, BC
V6B 2K4
Tel. 1-800-661-0020 (in BC, Alberta or Washington)
Tel. 1-800-663-5777 (rest of Canada) or (604) 684-7101
www.hihostels.bc.ca – online reservations available

Wilderness Accommodation
Many wilderness campsites operate on a first-come-first-served basis. However, there are currently 68 parks within British Columbia that do accept reservations. For a list and map of participating parks, or to reserve your campsite, call Discover Camping at 1-800-689-9025. Alternately, visit them online at www.discovercamping.ca. Provincial and national parks that are not listed do not accept reservations. See also 'Accommodation in Wilderness Areas' in the section 'On the Trail' and 'Camping in BC Parks' and 'Staying in National Parks' in 'The Great Canadian Wilderness'.

Visitor Centres
Visitor centres are located in most towns and all cities and are a great source of local information.

Tourism British Columbia
1117 Wharf Street
Victoria, BC
V8W 2X2
Tel. 1-800-663-6000
www.travel.bc.ca

National Parks

See 'Protected Areas: National and Provincial Parks' in section 'The Great Canadian Wilderness'. Anyone entering the national parks must purchase a pass at the gate of the park (see 'Great Western Annual Pass' in 'On the Trail').

Climate

The climate of British Columbia varies from continental to maritime, with the southern interior being the warmest and the driest; hence the fruitbelt in the Okanagan area. The whole coastal region of BC has a maritime climate – mild temperatures and lots of rain especially in winter. The interior is drier, but colder in winter and hotter in summer. Northern BC has cold winters and cool summers. In the Rockies, it is likely that the trails will be snow covered until July except at low elevations.

Money and Credit Cards

The Canadian currency is made up of dollars and cents. Paper bills are in the following denominations and colours: $5 (blue), $10 (purple), $20 (green), $50 (red), and $100 (brown). Coins come in $2 (twoonies), $1 (loonies), 25 cents (quarters), 10 cents (dimes), 5 cents (nickels) and 1 cent (pennies). Credit cards are widely accepted (Visa, Mastercard and American Express), and there are ATM bank machines in cities, towns and most places with commercial activity.

Time Zones

British Columbia has two time zones: the BC Rockies are on Mountain Time, which is GMT-07hours, and the majority of BC is on Pacific Time, which is GMT-08 hours. Daylight Saving Time is in effect from the first weekend in April until the last weekend in October.

Health Matters

No vaccinations are required to enter Canada. Visitors should have adequate medical and other insurance prior to arrival. Canada does not have a reciprocal health agreement with the UK, and hospital charges can be very expensive. Doctors will continue prescriptions that are issued in Europe, but it is best to bring supplies of any prescription used. The telephone number for emergencies is 911.

Mail/Post

Mail is delivered Monday to Friday. Retail postal centres can be found in every town or city, and, in addition to the post office, postal services can often be found in drugstores and corner stores such as 7–11.

Business Hours

Business office hours are generally Monday to Friday, 9am to 5pm. In cities, malls are often open until 9pm, especially Thursday and Friday nights, and are open Saturday until 5 or 6pm; some are open Sundays too. In smaller places, expect the shops to be shut at 5 or 6pm and closed on Sundays. Bars in most places are usually open until 2am. In BC, the legal drinking age is 19.

Telephones

In Canada, local calls are unmetered. Local calls from a payphone cost a quarter. Phone keypads have letters as well as numbers, and companies often have phone numbers that also contain letters: just dial in the normal way. Any numbers beginning with 1-800, 1-888, or 1-877 are toll-free. Toll-free numbers can be accessed from outside Canada (using the country code) , but a charge is made for these calls. The area code for Vancouver is 604 and the area code for the rest of BC is 250.

Electricity

Electricity voltage in Canada is 60 cycles, 110 volts. An adapter is required for all European appliances that are 220 volts.

Weights and Measures

Canada goes by the metric system.
1 kilometre = 0.62 miles

New poles stand proud at Qay'llnagaay, Haida Gwaii

1 mile = 1.609 kilometres
$1km^2$ = 1 hectare (ha) = 247 acres
1kg = 2.2lbs
1 litre = 1.057 quarts
1 yard = 0.9 metres
0°C= 32°F

Food and Drink

British Columbia is world-renowned, for its seafood especially its smoked salmon. It is often noted as being the California of Canada because of its health-consciousness, and smoking is prohibited in many restaurants, organic and vegetarian foods are plentiful, and coffee bars and cafes are on every street corner. There are lots of micro-breweries with different ales, lagers and ciders to sample – make sure to visit the Granville Island Brewery in Vancouver.

Tipping

Canada is one of those countries where tipping is expected, and especially at bars and restaurants the service staff depend on their tips for the majority of their income. So make sure to leave about 15%. For large groups, the gratuity is often added to the bill automatically.

Tax

In BC, a harmonized sales tax (HST) of 15% is applied to most purchases. This includes the goods and services tax (GST) of 7%, which is applied to most foods and services. Non-resident visitors are entitled to a rebate of GST on certain goods they take out of Canada and certain short-term accommodation. To apply for the rebate, save all receipts of purchases totalling more than $50 (before tax) and pick up the pamphlet 'Tax Refund Application for Visitors' to find out what purchases qualify. It can be found at any customs office, visitor information centres, airports, duty-free shops and some hotels.

Languages

Canada has two official languages – English and French – but there are lots of other cultures and languages represented in British Columbia, including a large Asian population and lots of different

First Nations groups. In Vancouver and Richmond especially, there are high percentages of Chinese immigrants.

Internet Access

It's relatively easy to find internet access all over BC, even in small rural areas. All Hostelling International hostels and most other hostels have internet kiosks for web and email access. There are internet cafes all over the place, and libraries often offer free time.

HOW TO USE THIS GUIDE

This book contains four main sections: 'On The Trail'; 'The Great Canadian Wilderness'; 'Equipment'; and the trail descriptions. 'On the Trail' gives all the practical information needed for hiking and camping in BC. 'The Great Canadian Wilderness' prepares the visitor for any dangers and hazards that might be encountered, such as wildlife, and offers advice on survival. The 'Equipment' section describes the equipment and clothing needed for specific environments, including first-aid kits, and offers suggestions for places to rent or buy equipment in BC. The trails section of the guide focuses on specific regions of British Columbia and trails found within them. This section is divided into chapters based on regions. Each chapter (and region) contains practical information, such as access to the region, transportation within it and local accommodation. There are sections on the cultural history and natural history. The trails within the particular region are further grouped under their applicable national, provincial or regional parks. All national park and most provincial park sections begin with natural or cultural history and general information such as campsite locations.

This guide contains a great mixture of walks with regards to region, distance and time. Some of the trails are day-hikes while others span over several days. Some of the longer treks are divided into several shorter sections that can be completed in a half-day or day. Some are divided according to the difficulty of certain sections to make the differences clear.

Maps

Topographic Maps

The Centre for Topographic Information of Natural Resources Canada is Canada's national topographic mapping agency (http://maps.nrcan.gc.ca). Their NTS (National Topographic System) maps are produced at a scale of 1:250,000 and 1:50,000. Both these are detailed maps showing landforms, terrain, lakes, rivers, forest cover, populated areas and transportation routes. The 1:50,000 maps are good for recreational use, and are suitable for hiking, cycling, canoeing and camping. The 1:50,000 maps cover an area of approximately 1000km². These maps are distributed to the public through regional distribution centres. Contact ITMB Publishing Ltd., 530 West Broadway, Vancouver, BC, V5Z 1E9, tel. (604) 879-3621, or visit the website: http://maps.nrcan.gc.ca/topographic.html. Topographic maps are often sold at visitor information centres as well as outdoor specialist shops.

Forest Service Recreation Maps

The BC Forest Service produces about 40 different maps at various scales that are available to the public. These maps show Forest Service campgrounds, hiking trails, interpretive forests and logging roads. They are available for purchase from local Forest Service offices and often visitor information centres as well. For a listing of what is available, check www.for.gov.bc.ca/hfp/rec/maps/svanisle/

Recreation Maps

Gem Trek Publishing Ltd specializes in producing detailed maps of the Canadian Rockies. These maps are 1:100,000 scale and there is one that covers Kootenay National Park and another that combines Lake Louise and Yoho National Park. These maps are very useful as they show ground relief, campgrounds, hiking trails and roads. These can be purchased locally, or contact: Gem Trek Publishing Ltd., Box 1618, #6- 245- 2nd Ave E, Cochrane, Alberta, T0L 0W0, tel. (403) 932-4208.

Using this Guide

In this guidebook there are location maps at the beginning of each

*Pole-raising
celebrations,
Qay'llnagaay,
Haida Gwaii*

trail chapter to show driving routes into and around the region as
well as trail maps that accompany the routes. The maps show the
suggested trails, alternative trails if applicable, major oceans, rivers
and streams, major towns, campsites, parking areas and park boundaries. These maps are drawn as a basic guide and are intended for
general orientation, but should in no way be used for route finding.
The appropriate NTS maps should be taken on all hikes in this wilderness country, and map details are given at the beginning of each trail.

   Each of the trail descriptions are preceded by a box containing
key information, which is explained below. For example:

Trail 1 Juan de Fuca Marine Trail

Distance: 47km, linear

Time: 3–5 days

Rating: moderate–difficult

Elevation: mainly sea level

Maps: NTS 92C/8, 92C/9

Base: Victoria or Port Renfrew

Best time: May–October

Tide Tables Needed

Distance

Distances are given in kilometres, and trails are designated as linear or circular.

Time

Time is given in hours or days, depending on whether the walk is a day-hike, overnight trip or multi-day trek.

Rating

The difficulty of each trail is rated for the average visitor. There are three basic categories: easy, moderate and difficult. An easy rating means that almost everyone can do the trail: it is short or flat with little elevation change. Easy trails are suitable for children. A moderate rating means the trail requires basic physical fitness and there may be a few terrain challenges. A difficult rating means that the trail requires a high level of physical fitness and backcountry knowledge. It might be a long trail or maybe just a steep one. So what might be rated moderate–difficult might present no difficulties for an experienced and physically fit mountaineer. Then again, some of the trails are very steep, so they are difficult for anyone. Never overestimate the abilities of the group, and you have any hesitation, it might be better to go with a guided group (see 'Guided Hikes' in section 'On the Trail').

Elevation

The elevation change is given at the beginning of each trail and should be considered in relation to the abilities of the group. A walk may only be a couple of kilometres but may climb 500m in this short distance.

Maps
The map references refer to the NTS maps that correspond with the trail and area (see 'Topographic Maps', above).

Base
BC is a big place, so the base given for the trails is usually the nearest town or city, or place with a hostel or a campground. The directions to the trailheads are given in the Access sections prior to the trail descriptions.

Best Time
This indicates the best time of year to visit. Many of the trails and roads in the Rockies are closed until the snow melts, which may be as late as July. Many of the coastal trails are simply too wet and muddy during the early spring months. Some trails are open year-round, but are best enjoyed when flowers are in bloom.

Tide Tables Needed
'Tide tables needed' indicates a coastal trail that traverses the beach for at least part of the trail. Tide tables are needed to time certain sections to avoid being cut off from the trail at high tide (see 'Tide Tables' in 'On the Trail' section).

Access
Access to the trailhead from the base town/city is given with each trail description. Some of the trailheads are easily accessible from a main highway, some from a series of gravel logging roads, while others require a short boat ride or water taxi.

Trail Conditions
Most of the routes in this book follow well-marked trails. Conditions on the trails may change from one part of the season to the next depending on rainfall, snowmelt, and so on. Check in at the park visitor centres for accurate and up-to-date trail conditions.

Wilderness scenery, British Columbia (photo Martijn Coini)

Alternatives

For some trails, alternatives are provided. These include longer or shorter versions of the trail, or simply suggest something else to do, such as canoeing instead of walking around a lake.

Appendices

The end of this guidebook contains several appendices: 'Vancouver'; 'Northwest Coast Native Cultures'; and 'Useful Addresses'. The Vancouver section is included because, although no trails are within the city district, most visitors to BC begin or end their trip in the metropolis. The appendix on Northwest Coast Native Cultures contains further sources of information for those interested both in the cultural history of BC and the strength of those cultures today. Helpful Addresses is a compilation of all useful addresses mentioned in the guide.

ON THE TRAIL:
PRACTICAL INFORMATION FOR
HIKING AND CAMPING

The walking trails in this guide take the hiker through a mixture of national and provincial parks, municipal recreation areas and forest districts. Twenty-two of the trails are within the park boundaries of five of British Columbia's six national parks. This section offers essential information on all the practicalities of walking the trails, including wilderness accommodation, park permits, driving on logging roads, how to use tide tables to plan a coastal hike and how to do a cable-car crossing. It also encourages ecotourism and environmentally responsible camping/hiking practices. The final portion deals with staying safe on the trail and rescue options.

Great Western Annual Pass

Anyone using Canada's national park system (see 'Protected Areas' in 'Great Canadian Wilderness' section) must obtain a pass that can be purchased at the gate of the park. Visitors spending any length of time, or visiting many parks, may wish to consider the Great Western Annual Pass. These can be purchased from the tollbooths at the parks' gates. In British Columbia, the pass is valid at Yoho National Park, Kootenay National Park, Glacier National Park, Mount Revelstoke National Park and Pacific Rim National Park Reserve. It is also valid in Alberta for Banff National Park, Waterton Lakes National Park, Jasper National Park, Elk Island National Park, Prince Albert National Park and Riding Mountain National Park. The pass is valid for one year from the month of purchase and includes a discount booklet worth more than $100. Current fees are available at www.parkscanada.gc.ca

Accommodation in Wilderness Areas

Camping
Discover Camping offers a reservation service for all provincial and

national park campgrounds in BC that accept reservations. Reservations can be made up to three months in advance and two days prior to your arrival. Note that not all campgrounds accept reservations, and all campgrounds may fill up fast. The maximum length of stay in most provincial parks is 14 nights per park. In Pacific Rim National Park, the limit is 7 nights within a 30-day period. The reservation service operates from March to October. Contact www.discovercamping.ca or tel. 1-800-689-9025 or (604) 689-9025.

Backcountry fees

A backcountry fee is payable at the trailhead. Fill out the short form available there, and keep part of it as a receipt (you may be asked to show this to a warden as proof of payment). Put the form and the fee in the self-registration envelope provided, and post this in the box at the trailhead.

Forest Service Campgrounds

BC Forest Service operates 1400 campgrounds throughout the province. Some 80% of the funds collected are re-invested in the local forest districts to assist in maintaining and improving recreation facilities. A camping pass is required and entitles a person, family or group of up to six to occupy one site. An Annual Camping Pass is valid for all Forest Service campgrounds for one year from April 1st to March 31st. Camping passes can be purchased from government agents and various vendors. Call ENQUIRY BC at 1-800-663-7867 for the nearest vendor. An online recreation brochure including a detailed listing of Forest District Offices and campgrounds is available at: www.for.gov.bc.ca/hfp/rec/brochure/index.htm.

Hostels, Huts and Lodges

The Alpine Club of Canada (ACC) is Canada's national mountaineering organization. They operate an extensive network of alpine and backcountry huts throughout the country. Accommodation ranges from isolated bivvy shelters at the base of remote mountains to log cabins with easy approaches. Reservations are necessary at all ACC facilities and can be made through the national office. Details of specific huts and facilities are included with the appropriate trail information.

Alpine Club of Canada
Indian Flats Road
PO Box 8040
Canmore, Alberta
T1W 2T8
Tel. (403) 678-3200
Fax (403) 678-3224
Email: alpclub@telusplanet.net

Driving on Logging Roads

Many of the trails and parks in the more remote areas of British Columbia are accessible only via active logging roads. These roads, although open to the public, are built primarily to handle heavy industrial traffic. Main logging roads are usually rough gravel or dirt roads – some very rough roads are passable only with a 4-wheel drive vehicle. Check road and travel conditions locally before heading out. Some roads may be closed to the public during periods of extreme fire hazard or industrial use or during the winter months.

These are some tips for safe driving on logging roads:

- Check vehicle and fuel level before departing.
- Drive with caution at all times.
- Logging trucks have the right of way. Pull over at the nearest turn-off or pull over to the right as far as possible.
- Drive with the headlights on at all times – dust can impair vision considerably.
- Do not pass any heavy equipment unless signalled to do so.
- Observe all signs and hazard warnings and drive only on roads deemed safe for general use.
- Drive slowly.
- Watch for fallen trees, rocks and wildlife on the road.
- Park vehicles well off the main road.
- Remember that logging trucks are very heavy and cannot stop as quickly as a car.

Wilderness scenery, British Columbia (photo Martijn Coini)

South Beach on Haida Gwaii

Pole-raising ceremony, Haida Gwaii

Tide Tables

For many of the coastal trails, tide tables must be used to avoid being trapped or cut off from the trail at high tides. Tide tables are also used to time river crossings, and night-time high tides should be considered when pitching tents on the beach! The tide tables for a particular area are usually posted at the trailhead and at nearby visitor centres, and they may be purchased at visitor centres, outdoor recreation shops, and fishing and camping supply shops. They are also available online at: www.lau.chs-shc.dfo-mpo.gc.ca/marees/produits/english/canada.htm. The Canadian Hydrographic Service annually publishes tide and current tables for all the different regions of Canada's coast. They are straightforward and easy to use. Each volume contains tidal information for every day of the year from seven different reference ports in the particular geographic region. The tides are given in standard time. From the first weekend of April until the last weekend in October, daylight savings time is in effect. Standard time can be converted to daylight savings time by adding one hour.

Example:

Day	Time	Ht/ft	Ht/m
1	0350	10.5	3.2
MO	1100	-0.1	0.0
LU	1820	11.0	3.4
	2315	8.6	2.6

The Day column gives the date, which is the 1st, and the day in English, MO (Monday), and in French, LU (Lundi). The Time column uses the 24-hour clock and refers to the successive high and low tides. For example, if these were the tide tables for June 1st, after converting to daylight savings time, at 7.20pm the height of the tide is 11ft or 3.4m. If a part of the trail is cut off at tides higher than 10ft, then it would be necessary to either camp for the night before this section or time the day accordingly to pass this section before high tide.

Cable-Car Crossings

Some of the backcountry trails in British Columbia have cable-car crossings over some of the rivers. These crossings are not difficult, but do require careful attention. Only two people and their gear can cross at one time. Make sure to keep all hands, fingers and hair away from the pulleys, and be careful on slippery platforms. Use the rope to pull the car close, and hold it steady to load in the gear first. Then carefully enter the car and stay seated. To cross the river, let the rope go and gravity will move the car down the rope to the middle of the river. Then, pull the rope hand-over-hand to reach the platform on the other side. Hold the rope so that the car is steady and flush with the platform and then unload all the gear carefully. Never bounce or sway while in the car and never tie the car up to the platform.

Guided Hikes
In the trail chapters, there are options given for guided hikes. These are a good opportunity for visitors who may not feel comfortable doing a hike on their own, and for those looking to share experiences with groups of people or who wish to see the area through the eyes of a local. Visitor centres and park headquarters are also good places to seek out local guides.

Equipment
For equipment sales and rentals see section 'Equipment' below.

Ecotourism
The International Ecotourism Society defines ecotourism as 'responsible travel to natural areas that conserves the environment and sustains the well-being of local people'. In general, it involves travellers questioning who would benefit from the choices they make. British Columbia has many remote areas and many self-sustaining communities. Many of these communities depend on tourism for their economic stability. For people choosing tour companies and guided options, this means choosing a local operator who employs local workers and uses local produce and locally owned accommodation (www.ecoisland.ca/eiproject/ is a website which focuses on ecotourism aspects of Vancouver Island's tourism industry and includes a directory for Vancouver Island communities). For example, if a traveller wanted to visit Haida Gwaii, why would they travel with a large company from Vancouver or Seattle, for example, when there are lots of companies in Haida Gwaii who obviously could provide a more

intimate and knowledgeable experience since it is their home? Remember that some companies have a more positive economic impact on the host destination than others.

For independent travellers, here are a few tips on how to be an ecotourist:

- Travellers should learn as much about the history, culture, language and natural environment of their destination prior to departure. Locals are more likely to interact with travellers who show knowledge, interest and respect for the place they are visiting.

- Travellers can help conserve the environment by making sure that their economic impact directly benefits the local community. This again goes back to the fact that travellers should question who directly benefits from their choices.

- Respect the privacy and dignity of others and be sensitive to local customs. Ask prior to photographing people. Respect archaeological and cultural sites.

- Consume local foods and use public transport or locally owned transport to maximize the amount of financial benefit to the host destination.

- Practise no-trace camping and hiking and protect fresh water sources.

- When viewing wildlife, keep as far away as possible and move quietly and slowly. Never come between a mother and its young.

- Leave no trace. Travellers should minimize the amount of disposable items they pack.

Ethics For Responsible Backcountry Travel
There are certain rules of etiquette for travellers using backcountry areas. Travellers should acquaint themselves with them and tread lightly to maintain the integrity of the places they are visiting.

Tread Lightly
- Stay on the trails. Taking shortcuts, detouring around muddy parts and trampling through meadows destroys plants and soil structure and increases erosion.

- In meadows and areas without designated trails, groups should spread out to minimize impact.
- Never approach or feed wildlife.
- On the seashore, try not to crush barnacles and other marine life in tidal pools.

No-Trace Camping

- Choose a campsite well away from the trail and water sources.
- In beach areas, camp above the high-tide line to reduce impacts and soil compaction in vegetated areas. Avoid camping in dunes if possible.
- Take extra care when camping in alpine and subalpine areas – these areas are extremely fragile due to extreme conditions and a short growing season. A tent left in the same place in an alpine meadow for a few days will damage all the plants underneath. The plants will probably not recover during the rest of the short summer.
- Use tent pads where provided.
- Guard against risk of forest fire, and always use a stove when in the forest (see 'Stoves and Fuel' in 'Equipment' section).
- When breaking camp, restore the area to its natural state. Leave nothing.

No-Trace Beach Campfires

Anyone who builds a beach fire should guard against the risk of forest fire and leave no unsightly evidence when they leave.

- Use only small pieces of driftwood that will burn down to ash. Never cut vegetation for fires.
- Light the fire on the beach away from big pieces of driftwood. Keep the fire small and never leave it unattended. Cooking pots can be rested on rocks.
- Before leaving the area, make sure the ashes are cold. Remove and take away for proper disposal anything that hasn't burned completely. If the charcoal doesn't crumble to ash, pack it out for the next fire.

Deer, with track marks

- Scatter the ashes and unused driftwood.
- Rinse any rocks used with seawater to remove as much of the blackening as possible. Replace the rocks on the beach.
- Restore the area to its natural state before leaving.

Rubbish

- Pack out everything that is packed in.
- Reduce the amount of waste by removing all unnecessary packaging prior to departure.
- Remember, a clean campsite is less likely to attract bears or other wildlife.
- Carry out even biodegradable items because some take months to degrade – even apple cores and orange peel are unlikely to decompose before the next hiker comes to the area.
- Burn food scraps or bag them and pack them out. Return fish entrails to the ocean.
- Do not bury rubbish – the ground will be disturbed by the digging and animals will dig it up and scatter it.

Sanitation

- Go at least 100m away from water sources and campsites. Bury waste and toilet paper 20cm below the surface so they will not be uncovered and will decompose quickly.
- On the beach, dig a hole 20cm deep close to the water intertidal zone. Cover after use and let the tide do the rest of the work.
- Only use toilet paper if absolutely necessary.
- If burning toilet paper, do so in the campfire, not in the forest, to reduce risk of forest fire.
- It is better to take away for proper disposal toilet paper and feminine hygiene products.
- Never urinate or defecate directly into water to help prevent the spread of infections.

Washing

- Beach: the best place to wash clothes, dishes and bodies is either the ocean or the brackish water at the mouth of a stream. Sand is effective for scrubbing dishes. Bring soap that works in salt water.
- Other: use a container for fresh water and do the washing at least

100m away from the water source. Use a small amount of phosphate-free soap.

- Do not pollute water sources in any way.

Safe Travel

- Be prepared – do not travel without appropriate maps, tide tables, equipment, clothing and food. Skills should include first aid, navigation and self-rescue techniques (see 'Rescue' below).
- Be aware that weather and travelling conditions can change quickly.
- Evaluate the fitness levels within the group before embarking on any major treks.
- Boil or treat all drinking water.
- Keep a distance from wildlife.

Respect

- Travellers should remember at all times that they are visitors in their host destinations.
- Respect all First Nations lands and policies.
- Obey all signs.
- Treat everywhere as a potential archaeological or cultural site – do not remove or disturb any artifacts, bones or cultural remains.

Rescue

AMBULANCE   tel. 1-800-461-9911

AIR OR MARINE EMERGENCY (Coast Guard) tel. 1-800-567-5111

FOREST FIRE REPORTING   tel. 1-800-663-5555

RCMP COASTAL WATCH   tel. 1-800-855-6655

- The **Canadian Coast Guard** is the rescue coordination centre for air and marine only.
- BC **Ambulance Service** provides pre-hospital medical care only and can be very expensive if not covered by medical insurance. When phoning them, make sure to specify accessibility of the road (2-wheel drive or 4-wheel drive) or wilderness site.

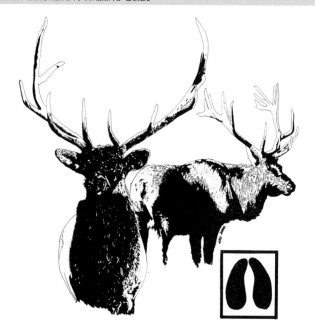

Elk, with track marks

- The **Royal Canadian Mounted Police** (RCMP) should be contacted in the event of missing persons. They control the activation of Search and Rescue, local resources and Provincial Emergency Program volunteers.

- Some of the western mountain national parks have **Parks Canada Technical Rescue Specialists** who provide emergency medical care and also have technical rescue expertise. Some national and provincial parks require anyone using the backcountry spaces to register with the park (this information is given with the applicable parks/trails).

Most of BC is not under Parks Canada jurisdiction. Rescues in most areas are conducted by the **Provincial Emergency Program (PEP)**. These are volunteers who are reimbursed only for food and travel expenses. Prevent unnecessary rescues by expecting the worst and being prepared. Common factors leading to problems are: inadequate clothing/equipment, inadequate skills, unexpected weather, poor judgement, injury or illness, and unexpected challenges such as snow, ice, currents, waves, etc. Simple things like dressing in layers, bringing extra food and water, and being aware of the limitations of the group can make all the difference.

Remember: many of the backcountry trails are remote wilderness where it may take up to 24 hours or more (particularly in adverse weather conditions) before help arrives if there is an accident.

Trip Plans

Trip plans can save lives. The chances of survival and rescue are significantly increased if a trip plan is given to a responsible person who knows who to notify if the hiker does not return when scheduled. Trip plan forms are available at many parks' offices or from Provincial Emergency Program (PEP) headquarters in Victoria (tel. 1-800-663-3456). Make sure to stick to the original plan or notify the designated person of any changes. And make sure to notify the designated person upon return.

Self-Rescue

Visitors planning to undertake hazardous trips or activities must realize that their safety is their own responsibility. The following self-rescue techniques could prevent the launch of expensive search and rescue operations that put a strain on local resources.

- Identify and avoid potential hazards.
- Ensure that all party members have some first-aid knowledge and basic competence in the environment/activity undertaken, and that they are properly equipped.
- Help others in the group.
- Be prepared to limp out with minor injuries, such as a sprained ankle.

THE GREAT CANADIAN WILDERNESS:
SAFETY AND SURVIVAL TIPS

Visitors come from all over the world to experience Canada's remote wilderness areas. Some are looking for adventure and excitement; others for solitude and serenity. Canada's parks and protected areas offer all of that because they remain 'wild' and seemingly untouched. These areas are home to grizzly bears and black bears, eagles and peregrine falcons, cougars and elk. Snow can come thundering down from the peaks of mountains in avalanches, the rocky coastlines are endlessly pounded with the roaring surf. Meanwhile, life goes on. This section details staying in BC's parks and surviving to tell about it!

PROTECTED AREAS – NATIONAL AND PROVINCIAL PARKS

Provincial Parks
BC has 637 provincial parks, recreation areas and ecological reserves. The Park Amendment Act in 1995 increased the total minimum area of the province to be designated as protected parks land from 2,550,000 to 7,300,000 hectares, which was further increased to 10,000,000 hectares in 2000. More than 200 parks have been created since 1991. Strathcona Park on Vancouver Island was established in 1911 and was BC's first provincial park. The Strathcona Park Act withdrew the lands from 'sale, settlement or occupancy.' By 1930, there were 13 provincial parks and at least 50 other areas were reserved for the pleasure and recreation of the public. In the early days, the parks were mostly used by the wealthy. Travel to the parks was by rail, accommodation was in private lodges and access within the parks was by foot or by horse. Although the main purpose of the Forest Service was to grow, protect and harvest trees, they also played an active role in parks and recreation, and they found that the parks' campgrounds were helpful in controlling forest fires by concentrating the public in specific areas. By 1957, the Department of Recreation

and Conservation was created in recognition of the distinction between park management and forest management. Its role was to establish, operate and manage provincial parks. In 1965, a revised Park Act acknowledged the need to establish parks for conservation purposes, not just recreation purposes.

Camping In BC Parks

Provincial Park campgrounds may have vehicle access or may be walk-in only campsites. There are a few regulations. Gates are open from 7am to 11pm, and it is advised to check in before 10pm. Quiet time is from 11pm to 7am. All pets must be kept on a leash, and pets are not allowed in the beach areas unless otherwise designated by a sign. No person is allowed to camp in a particular park for more than 14 days per calendar year. Some parks are open year-round and offer winter camping, but most are only open for the summer season. (See 'Camping' in 'On the Trail' section for reservations.)

National Parks

Canada's national parks protect representative examples of the Canadian landscape. Parks Canada has identified 39 natural regions across the country, and efforts to create new parks are concentrated on those areas without a park. To be a representative, the area must 'portray the geology, physiography, vegetation, wildlife, and ecosystem diversity characteristic of the region'. Also, the area's ecosystem must be in a 'healthy natural state or if they are stressed or significantly modified, the area must have potential for being restored to a natural state'. BC's national parks include: two parks in the Rockies – Yoho National Park and Kootenay National Park, which are both UNESCO World Heritage Sites; Glacier National Park, which protects lush interior rainforests and permanent glaciers; Mount Revelstoke National Park, which contains a rainforest of 1000-year-old cedars as well as its mountains; Pacific Rim National Park Reserve on Vancouver Island with its spectacular marine and mountain areas; and two in the Queen Charlotte Islands – Gwaii Haanas National Park Reserve, which protects Haida culture and coastal rainforest, and Gwaii Haanas National Marine Conservation Areas Reserve, which protects 138 of the Queen Charlotte Islands.

Staying In National Parks

Camping is available in all of BC's national parks except Mount Revelstoke (which offers only backcountry sites), and there are fire-places and firewood available at all of them. Hook-ups (electricity and sometimes sewage disposal) for Recreational Vehicles are only available at Kootenay National Park's Redstreak Campground. Pets are permitted, but must be on leashes at all times. Fishing is also available in all of BC's national parks: in Kootenay, Yoho, Glacier and Mount Revelstoke national parks, a national park fishing permit is required (available within the parks); and a federal tidal waters sport fishing licence is required in Pacific Rim and Gwaii Haanas national parks (available at government agents and local retail outlets). For more information on national parks, refer to www.parkscanada.gc.ca

SURVIVING IN THE WILD

British Columbia's wilderness areas can seem awesome and over-whelming to visitors who have never experienced such remoteness; they are equally as humbling. The following advice on dangers is not meant to scare off any potential visitors – it is simply to inform and remind people that they are not alone in the wilderness and that the forces of nature are often beyond our control and comprehension. Dangers may include animal encounters, slippery rocks or contami-nated drinking water. Armed with knowledge about hazards, hikers will be more alert and cautious and keep themselves out of harm's way. Survival often depends on being adequately equipped, having first-aid knowledge, using common sense and leaving a trip plan with someone reliable (see 'Trip Plans' in 'On The Trail').

Safety and Hazards

Many of British Columbia's backcountry trails are remote wilderness where it may take up to 24 hours or more before help arrives if there is an accident. To maximise the enjoyment of BC's outdoors, it is absolutely paramount that hikers be prepared for all weather condi-tions, be knowledgeable about first aid and be physically fit enough to do the trail they choose. They must also have navigational skills, the necessary maps and a compass. Portable electronic devices such

Cougar, with track marks

as a GPS or cell phone can create an illusion of safety and should never replace traditional route-finding skills. Hikers should never overestimate their abilities, and beginners or those with known knee, back, or ankle injuries should not attempt demanding hikes. During wet and rainy periods, occurrences of physical injury and hypothermia increase significantly.

Tides/Undertow/Rogue Waves
Many of BC's coastal trails offer the experience of both the tranquillity and the awesome and sometimes terrifying power of the ocean. It is always necessary to take caution around water. Assume all walking

surfaces to be slippery at all times, especially during rainy periods. Some creeks or rivers may have to be crossed by wading. Wait for safe water levels and low tides and undo the hip belt on your pack to allow for easy removal in case of slipping and falling. Tide tables should be used to plan the day on all coastal trails to avoid being cut off from the trail at high tide; high tides can make some beach walking either entirely impossible or very difficult. Be careful of undertows along the beaches and at river mouths and beware of rogue waves. These are unusually large waves that hit the beach every so often and are capable of pulling a person into the ocean.

Avalanche Safety

For winter recreation enthusiasts, knowledge of snow and avalanche safety is absolutely imperative in the Canadian wilderness. The Canadian Avalanche Association produces a telephone Avalanche Information Bulletin that provides up-to-date information for the Rocky Mountains, the South Coast Mountains, the South Columbia Mountains and the North Columbia Mountains. It is available free of charge to the public and is updated twice weekly at 1-800-667-1105. The Association also promotes and encourages avalanche safety training for all winter recreation enthusiasts through its Recreational Avalanche Course (RAC) programme. More information and a glossary explaining snow-, avalanche- and weather-related terms can be found on their website at www.avalanche.ca, or write to them at The Canadian Avalanche Centre, PO Box 2759, Revelstoke, BC, V0E 2S0, tel. (250) 837-2435.

Drinking Water

Consider all drinking water to be potentially contaminated with bacteria, viruses, fungi, protozoan cysts, worm eggs and other parasites. Treat all drinking water by boiling, filtering or adding iodine. British Columbia has problems with giardiasis – an infection that is caused by the parasite *Giardia lamblia* and transmitted through water that has been contaminated by the faeces of infected animals and people. On most of the trails, it is fairly easy to obtain water from streams; in cases where it's not, this fact has been highlighted with the trail. The best places to obtain water are fast-moving rivers, well water and the deepest part of lakes. Avoid stagnant water, shoreline water and water close to human habitations. Many campsites offer a tap with running water – this too should be treated before drinking. Bottled water will be readily available in the nearby towns, but don't expect to find any supplies or water at most park campsites.

Wildlife Hazards

Cougars: Attacks on people are rare, but children and crouching adults are most at risk. Never leave a child unattended, and avoid being alone on a trail at dawn or dusk. In the event of a cougar encounter, do not stare into the cougar's eyes, do not run and do not crouch down. Do pick up small children and back away slowly.

Elk: Elk can be aggressive and attack without warning. Males are particularly aggressive during the mating season (August to September) and during the calving season (May to June); females will aggressively defend their young. Do not approach an elk at any time.

Deer: Deer may aggressively seek food and may lash out with their hooves if they feel threatened. Do not approach or feed deer. It is best to leave dogs at home, as they have been known to provoke deer attacks on both animals and people.

Bison: Bison are dangerous and unpredictable and may charge without any warning. Keep at least 150ft away at all times, never approach them at the roadside and never come between two animals, especially a female and her calf. A bison can sprint at 50km/hr and weighs up to 2000 pounds.

Wood ticks: Wood ticks are mostly found in spring and early summer. They are parasites that live in tall grass and low shrubs and seek out warm-blooded hosts. They should be avoided, as they are potential carriers of disease. Wearing gaiters or tucking pants into socks can protect the legs. The best way to remove a tick is by grasping it and pulling up gently with tweezers. Disinfect the site with alcohol afterwards. If possible, save the tick in a small container so a doctor can look at it in case the area around the bite becomes infected or a fever develops.

Bear Safety

British Columbia is home to one quarter of Canada's black bears and half of Canada's grizzly bears. Black bears can be found all over the province, and grizzlies may be found in most places except

Black bear, with track marks

Vancouver Island and Haida Gwaii (although there are few, if any, in the heavily populated Vancouver and surrounding areas). Everyone should respect the fact that the wilderness areas are their homes and should help to conserve this habitat and the bears themselves.

Despite the vast numbers of visitors to backcountry areas of British Columbia, the number of human–bear encounters is low and attacks are very rare. When attacks do happen, it is usually the result of human carelessness. Prevention and awareness are the best methods of avoiding a bear encounter. The safety advice hikers will encounter everywhere in BC is not aimed to scare but rather to educate – for the safety of bears as well as people. The most dangerous bears are those habituated to humans and rubbish. When bears become habituated, they lose their fear of humans and usually end up in situations where they must be destroyed to protect the public interest. Help prevent this. The main things to remember are:

- respect all bears and remember that all bears are dangerous
- NEVER approach a bear
- NEVER feed a bear – it is illegal and dangerous to feed or intentionally attract a bear
- NEVER surprise a bear.

Facts About Bears
- Bears can run as fast as horses both uphill and downhill.
- Black bears and young grizzlies can easily climb trees.
- Bears have a very strong sense of smell and hearing and their eyesight is good.
- Bears are strong – they can easily tear apart a car or tent in search of food.
- Bears are strong swimmers.
- Bears aggressively defend their food.
- All female bears defend their cubs.
- Every bear defends a 'personal space'.
- Bears generally avoid contact with humans, but in rare cases may approach hikers.

So, when in bear country:
- be alert
- look for signs of recent bear activity – tracks, droppings, evidence of digging

Grizzly bear, with track marks

- make noise – talk loudly, sing, clap
- hike in groups
- keep children close
- stay away from dead animals
- leave dogs at home – dogs can antagonize bears and cause an attack

- reduce or eliminate odours – odours attract bears
- Store all food at least 4m above the ground – don't keep ANY food in the tent
- properly store and take away for proper disposal all rubbish
- do not sleep in the same clothes you cook in when camping
- cook at least 50m away from the tent.

Bear Encounters

- Never run away from a bear – they can run faster.
- Back away slowly and talk in a deep voice – raise arms to appear bigger.
- Always give the bear an escape route.

Bear Attacks

Aggressive bears are usually defending their territory, a fresh kill or their cubs. A predatory bear, however, is looking for food. How to respond depends on whether it is a grizzly bear or a black bear. In general, it is said 'if it has a hump (grizzly), act like a lump; if it's black, fight back'. If it is a grizzly bear, it is best to play dead as struggling may encourage an attack. People should drop to the ground and curl their knees up to their chest and put their hands behind their neck – this protects the head and all organs. If it is a black bear, fight back with anything possible – sticks, rocks, hands and feet.

EQUIPMENT

One of the key factors to a successful backpacking trip is having the proper equipment (and the knowledge of how to use the equipment). This involves pre-planning and learning as much about the destination as possible. Generally, the hiking season in BC is from May to September. This doesn't mean that people don't hike all year round – these are just the prime months to enjoy many different areas of the province. Spring is usually wet and muddy on the trails; summer can be hot and some areas may have lots of bugs; and in the autumn it starts to get cool again. Mountain parks usually open late spring and some trails may be snow-covered until July. Some people do camp in the winter, but this requires special equipment geared for cold temperatures, snow and winds, and also requires a lot of backcountry experience. The equipment described in this section is mainly for hikers/campers during the peak season – May to September. Hikers should be prepared for a range of temperatures (layering clothes is best) and climate conditions such as sun, rain, wind and possibly hail or snow.

Boots
Invest in a quality pair of sturdy hiking boots with good ankle and arch support. Boots with good traction on slippery surfaces are best. The difference between a pair of warm, dry, comfortable boots and a pair of flimsy, poor-quality ones cannot be overstressed. In most cases with boots, you get what you pay for. Don't wait until the beginning of a five-day trek to break in new boots; wear them as much as possible beforehand. Sandals and sneakers are good to wear around camp or for river crossings.

Pack
Backpacks should have a padded hip belt and shoulder straps, and be lined with a waterproof liner or rubbish bag. Good cushioning on the pressure points will help to reduce friction and blisters. Carrying too much weight is one of the most common mistakes a hiker can make, and can turn an otherwise great trip into a grueling punish-

ment. The new generation of packs are adjustable, thus making them far more comfortable than older-style packs – ask the salesperson to help adjust it to the perfect fit. In general, no one in the group should carry more than 25% of their body weight.

Tent

A tent with a good waterproof fly is necessary. Choosing a tent depends on how, where and when it will be used. Weight is the main factor for backpackers, while space might be a bigger factor for those camping only at vehicle-accessible sites. A three-season backpacking tent is constructed to be lightweight, compact and easy to assemble. A four-season mountaineering or expedition tent is designed to withstand high winds and snow. In general, a dome-shaped tent will be more aerodynamic and stable in a high wind. When weight is not a factor, a larger cabin-style tent might be preferable for families looking for comfort and using their tent as a base from which to explore (rather than backpacking).

Sleeping Bag

There are three main things to consider when buying a sleeping bag – shape, filling material (synthetic or down) and temperature rating. A mummy shape will pack smaller, while a rectangular shape allows for more movement. A synthetic-filled bag is less expensive, is good for those who are allergic to down, will continue to insulate even when wet and dries quickly. Down is the best natural insulator. Down-filled bags are lighter and pack smaller but are more expensive (although they have a longer life). Since down is useless when wet and dries slowly, look for a bag with a shower-proof fabric. Sleeping bags are rated for their insulating properties and take into account the use of a Thermorest or sleeping pad. Sleeping pads provide extra insulation against the cold ground. Choose a sleeping bag that suits the activity, location and time of year – for example a bag suitable for tropical weather will not be warm enough for alpine camping, and, similarly, a winter bag will cause excess sweating in tropical conditions.

Stoves and Fuel

Campfires are not permitted in many areas; they may not be safe in places at risk of forest fire or they may not be environmentally responsible. Fire regulations will be posted at the trailhead or along the trail. In many areas, such as a winter rainforest or above the snowline, a campfire may simply not be possible. In stormy and wet weather, a campfire cannot be relied upon. Hikers and campers in British Columbia will need a good lightweight backpacking stove and fuel. Liquid gas in canisters (white gas, butane, propane) is easy to find around British Columbia in outdoor specialist stores, hardware stores and even some general stores in more remote areas. Some stores, like Mountain Equipment Co-op, will accept used canisters for recycling.

Clothing

The problem of dressing for different levels of activity, changing temperatures and unpredictable weather can be alleviated by simple layering techniques. Clothing can always be removed throughout the day; it cannot be added if it's not there. The base layer should keep the skin comfortable and dry. The insulation layer should trap and retain body heat providing extra warmth. The outer layer should protect against the elements: wind, rain, snow and sun.

- **Rain gear** – BC gets lots of rain, and good waterproofs are absolutely necessary in any season.
- **Warm gear** – it's a matter of personal preference, but fleece and wool are both good insulators. Fleece is the most popular choice because it wicks moisture, dries quickly and insulates even when it's wet. Wool is a good insulator even when wet, but it dries slowly and becomes heavy (and slightly smelly) when wet.
- **Base layer** – under-layers should be warm and quick drying even when wet; synthetic fibres are preferable to cotton and silk for high activity because these natural fibres dry slowly, cooling the body (cotton keeps the body cool in tropical weather).
- **Hats** – one hat to shield the sun (even in winter, the sun can be hazardous especially in the mountains) and another for warmth (even in summer, nights can be cold, especially on the coast or in the mountains).
- **Gaiters** – these are especially useful on wet coastal trails for keeping mud and sand out of boots.
- **Gloves/mitts**.

- **Socks** – inner and outer layers – (see 'Note on Blister Prevention' below).

Other Camping Equipment

- **Watch** – absolutely necessary to time the tides on coastal trails.
- **Flashlight** – bring a reliable, compact, waterproof flashlight with spare batteries.
- **Knife** – a good pocket knife has a million uses; have it handy at all times.
- **Waterproof matches/lighter**.
- **Compass** – carry a compass and learn how to use it properly.
- **Tide tables** – essential on coastal trails to time hiking and avoid being cut off from the trail at high tides.
- **Map** – it isn't necessary to carry huge topographic maps for a short day-hike, but some type of trail and area map is important to have at all times. Carry it in a waterproof pouch along with the tide tables.
- **First-aid kit** – a basic kit should contain different sized sticking plasters, antiseptic wipes, sterile pads, burn cream, pain reliever (aspirin, etc), gauze, tape, tweezers, insect-sting relief and blister treatment. For longer backcountry hikes, see the first-aid kit list below and make sure someone in the group has proper training.
- **Water** – this is probably the heaviest thing to carry, but absolutely vital for hikers. 1–2 litres is the absolute minimum per day required for drinking (more in hot weather or on strenuous trails, plus extra for cooking). Dehydration can be a real threat to hikers – fill water bottles before the trip and refill whenever possible (note that all drinking water should be treated). Take frequent water breaks – the body is already 1% dehydrated at the first feeling of thirst.
- **Sunglasses and sunscreen**.
- **Food** – necessary for refuelling, but also carry extra for emergencies. Take foods that are lightweight and high in carbohydrates and protein. Leave as much of the packaging at home as possible.
- **Cooking utensils**.

- **Insect repellent**.
- **Rope** – 50m of rope per group to hang food, clothes to dry, etc.
- **Rubbish bags** – to take away for proper disposal rubbish and keep things dry.
- **Water treatment**.
- **Whistle** – a good survival whistle should be worn around your neck, not in a pack.
- **Waterproof pen/pencil**.
- **Survival bag or blanket** – can be used as a shelter from wind, rain and snow as well as for warmth.

First-Aid Kit for Backcountry Hikes

- Aloe Vera gel – for sun and wind burn, rashes, abrasions, minor burns and small wounds (accelerates healing)
- Antiseptic towelettes
- Latex gloves
- Sterile needle for draining blisters and removing slivers
- Razor – for shaving area to apply tape and close wound
- Safety pins to secure bandage ends
- Scissors
- Sterile scalpel blade for removing dead skin – ie. broken blisters
- Splint
- Syringe for wound irrigation
- Thermometer
- Tweezers
- Tick pliers to remove ticks easily
- Wire saw
- Bandages
- Sticking plasters
- Wound closures
- Burn/blister dressing
- Gauze

Yoho National Park

Note On Blister Prevention

Keep skin dry – choose socks that keep the feet slightly cool to reduce the amount of sweating. Synthetic inner socks will wick moisture away and keep the layer closest to the skin dry. If boots are wet, wear plastic bags over dry socks.

Eliminate friction – make sure boots fit properly and break them in slowly. Wear two layers of socks. Note that hiking uphill and hiking downhill produces different friction spots. Uphill puts pressure on the heel as the foot slips back, and downhill irritates the toes and soles as the foot slips forward. Many hiking boots have a cleat which enables two separate tensions between the upper and lower. When hiking uphill, tighten the upper portion of the boot and loosen across the foot. For downhill, loosen the upper part of the boot and tighten across the foot.

Equipment Sales/Rentals

West Coast Trail Express

The West Coast Trail Express is a charter bus service on Vancouver Island, and it also has equipment for rent and for sale. In the way of hiking gear, they have backpacks, tents, sleeping bags, rain gear, fuel, cooking equipment, gaiters, Gortex gear and Thermorests. They also rent out storage space to store other gear while out on the trails. Kayaks and canoes can be rented and delivered to Victoria, Port Renfrew or Bamfield, or phone to arrange another location.

West Coast Trail Express Inc.
3954 Bow Road
Victoria, BC V8N 3B1
Tel. (250) 477-8700
Email: wcte@pacificcoast.net

Mountain Equipment Co-op

Mountain Equipment Co-op is one of Canada's biggest outdoors stores, with several locations across the country. It operates as a co-operative, which means anyone wishing to buy something must become a member, but the cost is only about $5 and it's worth it.

Besides having a great selection of quality equipment to buy, they also rent out gear, including sleeping bags, tents, 70L packs, canoes, kayaks, climbing gear, skis and snowshoes. Reservations can be made up to one month in advance, and one day's rental fee can be deducted from the purchase of the same equipment within 30 days of rental. The BC shop is located in Vancouver at:

Mountain Equipment Co-op
130 West Broadway
Vancouver, BC
V5Y 1P3
Tel. (604) 872-7858
www.mec.ca

Sports-Rent
Sports-Rent is Victoria's complete sports rental centre. It's open seven days a week and they occasionally have massive sell-offs of their ex-rental gear. They rent out mountain bikes, hiking/camping equipment, tents, surfboards and wetsuits, roof racks and boats.

Sports-Rent
611 Discovery Street
Victoria, BC
V8T 5G4
Tel. (250) 385-7368
www.sportsrentbc.com

VANCOUVER ISLAND

Cape Scott
Provincial
Park

Port Hardy

*STRAIT
OF
GEORGIA*

N

*PACIFIC
OCEAN*

Strathcona
Provincial
Park

Flores
Island

Tofino

Nanaimo

Pacific Rim National Park

Port
Renfrew

*Juan de Fuca
Strait*

Juan
de Fuca
Provincial
Park

Victoria

East Sooke
Regional
Park

BRITISH
COLUMBIA

0 10 20 30 40 50

Scale in kilometres

VANCOUVER ISLAND

Background

Vancouver Island has always been a draw for visitors to British Columbia. From the charm of Victoria to interior parks with lakes and mountains and waterfalls, to the rugged and harsh west coast, there is something to suit every taste. Vancouver Island boasts one of the most bountiful and diverse intertidal zones in the world, coastal lowland forests, temperate rainforests with towering trees, sandstone cliffs, sea arches, endless sandy beaches, rocky shorelines and an environment that is rich in both natural and cultural heritage.

Getting There

By Ferry: BC Ferries runs a service between Vancouver and Victoria, and Vancouver and Nanaimo. Departures for Victoria leave from Tsawwassen, just south of Vancouver (about 45mins from city centre – 'downtown'), and arrive at Swartz Bay, about 30 minutes north of Victoria. Crossing time is 1hr 35mins. During the summer months expect long waits, even though ferries run almost every hour from 7am until 9pm daily; the new reservation service should alleviate this. Vehicle spaces can be booked by calling 1-888-724-5223 within BC or (604) 444-2890 from outside (payment by credit card). The ferries take cars, RVs, buses, trucks, bicycles and foot passengers. The ferry from Vancouver to Nanaimo leaves from Horseshoe Bay and takes between 1hr 20mins and 1hr 35mins depending on which ferry it is. Crossings are less frequent than for Victoria, but during summer months there are about eight or nine a day. Schedules and current fares information can be obtained at any visitor information centre or hotel, or at www.bcferries.com

NB. For the hikes on the southern west coast (ie. Juan de Fuca Marine Trail or West Coast Trail), it's easiest to travel from Victoria. For Strathcona Park, Cape Scott, Flores Island and Tofino/Long Beach, take the Nanaimo ferry.

By Bus: Pacific Coach Lines runs a service between downtown Vancouver and downtown Victoria, and picks up at major hotels as well as the airports and cruise ship terminals. A one-way ticket includes the price of the ferry as well. Call 1-800-661-1752 or find them at www.pacificcoach.com

By Air: For visitors spending most of their time on the island, a ticket to Victoria is only a bit more than one to Vancouver, and the extra cost is equal to or less than the price of the ferry. A more expensive option for travel between Vancouver and Victoria is to fly. Air Canada, Canadian Airlines and Canada 3000 all operate flights. Or for some added excitement, Harbour Air (1-800-665-0212) offers a harbour-to-harbour seaplane service leaving from Waterfront Rd. West, downtown Vancouver or from the south airport terminal. Helijet Airways flies harbour-to-harbour in a 12-passenger helicopter (call (604) 273-1414).

Getting Around

It's easy to get around Vancouver Island. Laidlaw Coach Lines provides an excellent bus service connecting the island communities. For fares and schedules, check out www.victoriatours.com or contact: Gray Line of Victoria, 700 Douglas Street, Victoria, BC, V8W 2B3, tel. (250) 388-5248 or 1-800-663-8390. The West Coast Trail Shuttle Bus connects Victoria and Nanaimo to both the Juan de Fuca Trail and the West Coast Trail. For information and reservations, contact: West Coast Trail Express Inc, 3954 Bow Road, Victoria, BC, V8N 3B1, tel. 1-888-999-2288 or (250) 477-8700, email: wcte@pacificcoast.net

Driving Distances

Victoria to Port Renfrew	107km
Nanaimo to Tofino	206km
Victoria to Tofino	316km
Nanaimo to Port Alberni	84km
Victoria to Port Alberni	195km
Nanaimo to Bamfield	179km
Victoria to Bamfield	290km
Nanaimo to Port Hardy	391km
Victoria to Port Hardy	502km
Nanaimo to Holberg	435km
Victoria to Holberg	546km

Victoria Accommodation

Being the capital of BC and a city of about 300,000, there are hotels, B&Bs, motels and guesthouses to fit every budget, from full luxury down to the bare necessities. In any given place, it's easy to find a great expensive hotel, but harder to seek out a good budget one. Here are a couple:

Selkirk International Guesthouse
934 Selkirk Avenue, Victoria, BC V9A 2V1
(250) 389-1213

More in the style of a B&B, Norm and Lyn Jackson operate the guesthouse within their heritage home in west Victoria. Rooms are in the big house overlooking the river, complete with a dock, hot tub and trampoline. It offers lovely rooms, friendly people and lots and lots of character.

BC Ferries to Vancouver Island (photo Martijn Coini)

Hostelling-International Victoria
516 Yates Street, Victoria, BC V8W 1K8
(250) 385-4511
victoria@hihostels.bc.ca

Located in downtown Victoria, this hostel is right where it's all happening. With lots of perks like lockers, a very big kitchen, an intercom, an incoming courtesy phone and internet access, this is a popular, so somewhat crowded, yet incredibly friendly hostel.

JUAN DE FUCA PROVINCIAL PARK

Background
The west coast of Vancouver Island is shared by the Nuu-cha-nulth, 'All along the mountains' people, a contemporary alliance of 14 tribes, as well as the Pacheenaht, 'People of the sea foam', and the Makah, who aren't members of the alliance at the present time. On a political map, each village might be represented by a tiny dot on a fragmented coast (or not at all), but in reality each community represents a people. Each group has its own territory extending inland as far as the salmon go up the streams, as far up the mountains as the people go for cedar and as far out to sea as it is possible to go and still see the mountains. The history of these peoples began long before European colonization, which resulted in the disappearance of whole nations through disease, the destruction of indigenous culture and the almost complete extinction of coastal marine resources.

The history of this area and of the peoples who have lived here over centuries bustles with visitors. Their legends and stories tell of the Beachkeeper who was responsible, on behalf of the chief, for welcoming visitors. After a storm, the Beachkeeper might be lucky enough to find Ma'ak on his beach, the grey whale who travelled the coast from Mexico to the Bering Sea and back again every year. Whales and seals travelled great distances from their own worlds, where they took human forms. The Nuu-chah-nulth, Pacheenaht and Makah had highly sophisticated marine technology, and were the only people on the northwest coast to hunt whales in the open sea.

Tow Hill (Trail 15)

Shadow Lake (Trail 20)

Wild flowers in Mount Revelstoke National Park

Devil's Club
(*Oplopanax horridum*)
(photo Martijn Coini)

Giant Cedars in Mount Revelstoke National Park

The Kootenay Valley

Marble Canyon in Kootenay National Park

They are famed canoe builders, who carved the large cedar trees from the rainforest into great sea-going vessels. Preparation for the whales' arrival was intricately woven into every aspect of daily life. Two or three whales a year brought thousands of litres of oil, prestige and many guests at potlatches (ceremonies). For hunters, who were also chiefs, there was *osemitch*: spiritual and practical training for those who would face many dangers. This included meditation, prayer, fasting, swimming in icy seas and ritual diving to underwater caves. Legends also tell of the Thunderbird, who announced his presence with a thunderous clapping of his wings, and whom Hiyitliik, the fire-spitting serpent, often accompanied. Raven, Deer and others who possessed human qualities, transformed into the 'real' people of the complex society that came to be.

In 1774, a storm kept the Spanish from landing (although not from laying claims!), and in 1778 the Mowachat, 'People of the deer', guided Captain Cook away from a reef and into their harbour at Yuquot. He was greeted by the word 'nootka', as they were yelling at him to circle around the rocks, but he mistook it for their name, and called the other Nuu-chah-nulth peoples that as well. He then proceeded to claim the sovereign territories of 30 hereditary chiefs for Britain. The Spanish and the British signed the Nootka Convention, averting a war, and the Spanish withdrew. At the same time, the Mowachaht were swamped with Europeans wanting to buy up sea-otter pelts. By the early 1800s sea otters were nearly extinct, to be followed by the fur seals and then the whales, which were hunted by the thousands by huge commercial ships in the 1900s. And then, the nations began to disappear.

Since the 1980s, the Nuu-chah-nulth, Pacheenaht and Makah have been striving for more control and protection over what's left of their resources: their forests, salmon fisheries and their cultures. The Pacheenaht see part of their future in tourism, and run the ferries on the West Coast Trail, bus links from the trailheads, as well as the Pacheenaht Campground that offers hikers hot showers and towels as they leave the trail.

The Trail

The Juan de Fuca Marine Trail is located between Port Renfrew and Jordan River, just south of the West Coast Trail. Both trails had their

Vancover Island (photo by Martijn Coini)

origins in the 1889 telegraph line constructed between Victoria and Bamfield, but because the southern part didn't form part of the Life Saving Trail, as the West Coast Trail did, it disappeared for many decades. The coastline of the West Coast Trail is an area so treacherous that it was named 'the Graveyard of the Pacific' by European sea captains in the late 1880s. The Pacheenaht were the first coast guards along this area, and many a shipwrecked survivor was saved from the icy swells and taken to safety in their seaworthy canoes. In the 1970s, the Victoria Sierra Club started lobbying the provincial government to preserve the southern coast along the Juan de Fuca Strait. At the same time, Alex Merriman, a columnist for the *Victoria Colonist*, began promoting the preservation of Botanical Beach and other coastal areas, and the Sierra Club launched exploratory forays into the bush to try and link up some of the more popular beaches. Unfortunately, logging companies began harvesting the areas around Sombrio Creek and Parkinson Creek, destroying precious virgin forest. In the 1990s, the provincial government finally acquired the land base for the present-day trail. The trail was created in 1994 as a legacy of the Victoria Commonwealth Games; preservation of a living legacy was considered a fitting tribute to the spirit of the Games, and in 1995 the provincial government set it aside as a provincial park. The trail is 47km long and runs parallel to Highway 14; its construction was a collaboration of government, local industries and local citizens.

Access

The Juan de Fuca Marine Trail can be accessed by vehicle from Highway 14 at four trailheads: Botanical Beach, Parkinson Creek, Sombrio Beach and China Beach. China Beach is the closest to Victoria (about 1hr 15mins to drive), just past Jordan River. Botanical Beach is at Port Renfrew. The trail description is from Botanical Beach to China Beach, but the trail can be hiked either way or from any trailhead, offering unlimited day-use or multi-day hiking opportunities. The West Coast Trail Express Shuttle Bus (tel. (250) 477-8700) operates from Victoria to the West Coast Trail and will stop at the Juan de Fuca trailheads by request. It can also be flagged down on the highway. Without two cars to shuttle between trailheads, one option is to take the bus from trailhead to trailhead. Park at China Beach and take the shuttle to Port Renfrew, leaving the vehicle at the end of the trail. Parking is free, but don't leave any valuables in your car, as thieves are around and target rental cars or cars with foreign plates. From China Beach, it is just over 40km to Port Renfrew on a winding road that narrows to one lane in some areas. Port Renfrew is a small village with about 400 people that has some accommodation, stores and restaurants. The West Coast Trail Express Shuttle Bus doesn't drive all the way to Botanical Beach, but it's an easy 2.5km walk up a gravel road; alternatively, the shuttle driver knows a local guy who will drive hikers up for $5.

Port Renfrew Accommodation

The Port Renfrew area offers hotels/motels and B&B as well as camping. The Pacheedaht Beach Campground (tel. (250) 647-0900) has wilderness camping for $8, with a picnic area, beach, boat launch and showers.

TRAIL 1: JUAN DE FUCA MARINE TRAIL

Distance:	47km
Time:	3–5 days
Rating:	moderate–difficult
Elevation:	mainly sea level
Maps:	NTS 92C/8, 92C/9
Base:	Victoria or Port Renfrew
Best time:	May–October

Tide tables needed

Botanical Beach to Payzant Creek 7km
Easy–Moderate

At the Botanical Beach trailhead, there are self-registration envelopes and a red vault where hikers must deposit their camping fees ($5 per night per person – cash only). Keep the receipt and ticket portion, as a park warden will collect it along the way. There are fines for not paying. There are out-house toilets here as well as an information board that has a map of the trail, a more detailed map of Botanical Beach trailhead, tide tables and safety information on bears, cougars, packing out your rubbish, and so on. The trail starts or ends here at the trail marker for 47km. A short easy walk (1km) through the forest leads to Botanical Beach, which is famous for its plankton-rich tidal pools. At low tide, these pools teem with an abundance of marine life, including starfish, anemones and crabs. To maximize viewing opportunities, check the tide tables and be here when tides are less than 1.2m (4ft). This area is a protected zone and it's illegal to handle or take any wildlife. Orange balls hanging from trees mark the way off the beach back to the trail. The next 3km has boardwalks over most of the wet sections that have been built by the T'souke and Pacheedaht First Nations. The boardwalks, cut logs and seemingly easy sections of the trail can be very dangerous and slippery when wet, so wear proper boots and use caution at all times. The trail traverses through mature cedar-hemlock forest and there are informational signposts describing lichens and other plant and animal life

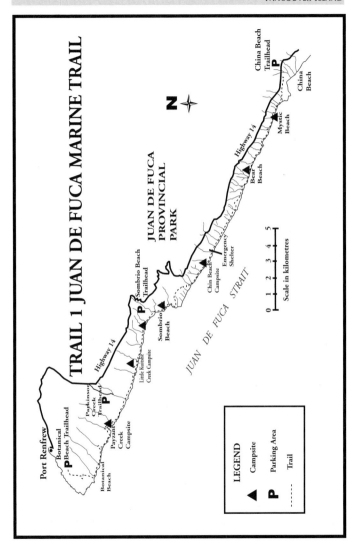

TRAIL 1 JUAN DE FUCA MARINE TRAIL

Port Renfrew

Botanical
Beach Trailhead

P

Botanical
Beach

Payzant
Creek
Campsite

Parkinson
Creek
Trailhead

P

Highway 14

Little Kuitshe
Creek Campsite

Sombrio
Beach

Sombrio Beach
Trailhead

P

JUAN DE FUCA
PROVINCIAL
PARK

N

Chin Beach
Campsite

Emergency
Shelter

JUAN DE FUCA STRAIT

Bear
Beach

Highway 14

Mystic
Beach

China Beach
Trailhead

P

China
Beach

LEGEND

▲ Campsite

P Parking Area

----- Trail

0 1 2 3 4 5

Scale in kilometres

found here. The trail crosses Tom Baird Creek at its mouth over logs. This is the easiest part of the trail with few elevation changes. A steel girded bridge crosses Soule Creek. At the 41km marker, the main trail reaches Providence Cove with a short side-trail leading to it. Further on, a sturdy log bridge crosses over Yuah Creek. After another 1km, the trail reaches Payzant Creek Campsite, which is a great place to stop for the day. There is an out-house toilet, campsites marked out by wooden squares and pulley-style hangers to hang food away from bears. An information board has a detailed map of the trail, the camp-sites, tide tables and safety information. Campsites are available at the top of a cliff overlooking the bridge across Payzant Creek with a great view of the waterfall. This is one of only two forest campsites on the trail, in the thick of lush greenery, so enjoy!

Payzant Creek to Little Kuitshe Creek 7km
Moderate
Those who started out early may wish to continue on to Little Kuitshe Creek during the first day; for others, this will be day two. The trail continues through the forest over lots of planks and boardwalks. The forest canopy is so dense here that not many species can survive. It is necessary to climb over a lot of tree roots, stumps and logs – a bit more climbing than the first section. At 39km, the trail enters a clear-cut area. This section is second-growth forest that was logged in the 1980s. The coast is accessible via several short side-trails. Near 38km hikers are able to walk along the shelf and explore tidal pools. In the autumn and winter, California and Stellar sea lions can be seen. Harbour seals are also very common. In the spring, after they've had their pups, the mother will place her newborn on the rocks while she goes fishing. Often seals can be seen basking in the sun on the rocks. The trail goes back into the forest inland and climbs over logs and fallen trees. In the summer, this area is full of berries and is feeding ground for black bears. Be alert and make lots of noise. The trail turns onto an old logging road, crosses a bridge over Parkinson Creek and leads to the Parkinson Creek trailhead. There's parking, a toilet and an information post here. A 3km gravel road leaves from the parking area back to the highway. It's another 3km through more new-growth forest to Little Kuitshe Creek at 34km. There is a waterfall just downstream of the bridge and for those feeling adventurous, it is only a short scramble down the left side and

quick wade across the creek to reach Kuitshe Cove with its small gravel beach. The Little Kuitshe Creek Campsite is 1km further. There's a trail that leads down to the coast from here with a good view of Sombrio Point. Campsites are in the forest and no fires are permitted.

Little Kuitshe Creek to Sombrio Beach East 6km
Moderate
The trail continues through second-growth forest. About 0.5km into the trail, it passes through a grassy bit. If it is high tide, the roaring surf can be heard in the sea caves below the shelf. A suspension bridge crosses Minute Creek upstream. Just past Minute Creek, there is access to the shore, and hikers may either hike the shoreline on the rocky shelf or else continue on the trail. The trail passes through another area of salal shrubs. Watch out not to trip over the roots that cross the trail, and be on alert for bears, especially in late summer when the berries are ripe. Soon the trail will approach the first of the points on the route that may be impassable by the tides. Check the tide tables before beginning the day and plan accordingly. The trail first reaches the extreme west side of Sombrio Beach, which is passable below 3m (9.8ft). About 0.5km down the beach is Sombrio Beach West (passable below 2.6m (8.5ft)). Sombrio is a large cobble beach with giant pieces of driftwood in all shapes. It's popular with surfers, particularly in the winter. Just before Sombrio River, there are a few wooden tent pads amidst the trees just off the beach. Fires are allowed on the beach but only above the high-tide line. A suspension bridge crosses over the river to the Sombrio Beach trailhead. The left fork of the trail leads to the parking area, the right continues the trail passing a private cabin. The trailhead map shows that there is a small parcel of private land. There used to be a whole community of squatters along the entire stretch of Sombrio Beach living peacefully until they were evicted in 1997. The trail heads through the forest a short way and then back to the coast to Sombrio Beach East at the trail marker for 28km (passable below 3m). This is a great place to camp and a good place to view marine life – sea lions, grey whales and orcas. From February to May, hikers may be lucky enough to see the migration of the grey whale – 17,000 of them travel up and down the coast and some spend the summer off the coast of Vancouver Island. There are no designated campsites but camp on the beach above the high-tide line.

Sombrio Beach East to Chin Beach 6km
Difficult

From here to Bear Beach is the most difficult part of the trail, and is best divided into two sections. The trail hugs the shoreline and climbs to Sombrio Point. From here, the trail turns inland to join up eventually with an old logging road at about 25km, and then slowly heads back to the coast. This part is difficult because of the elevation changes; there is a lot of climbing and descending in order to cross the many small streams. There is a suspension bridge that crosses Loss Creek, and from here there are great views out to the ocean and the beautiful sea stacks or, in the opposite direction, to a deep rocky gorge. The trail then follows the coastline and between 23 and 22km; hikers can choose to take the access trail and walk along the rocky area if it is low tide. Along the trail a bit further, there are numerous other beach access trails. Pay attention to the tide tables because Chin Beach is passable only below 2.75m (9ft). Here, there's a campsite, toilets and an information board. Just a little further east (at about 20km), there is a well-equipped emergency shelter that can sleep up to four. This cabin is especially useful in situations when hikers coming in the opposite direction get trapped by the tides and can't make it to the campsite.

Chin Beach to Bear Beach 12km
Most Difficult

This will be the most difficult section of the trail, so make sure to sleep well the night before. From the campsite, walk along the beach at low tide, passing the emergency shelter that is just inside the forest. The trail ascends and goes through a forest of mainly western red cedar, Douglas fir, hemlock and Sitka spruce. Again there is a lot of climbing and descending through creek drainages and headlands. During the rainy season, it can be exceptionally muddy. There are a few glimpses of the coast, but the trail is mainly through forest. The trail passes Magdalena Point between 14 and 13km, although it can't be seen from the trail. A bridge crosses Hoard Creek, and there is a beach access trail that leads down to a small gravel beach which floods at high tide. Just past the 10km marker, the difficult part is almost over and Bear Beach is just a short walk further. Just east of Ledingham Creek (around 10km), there is a campsite and pit toilet.

Bear Beach is passable only below 3m (9.8ft). At high tides, the ocean reaches the base of the cliffs and cuts off the west from the east. The best place to camp is at Clinch Creek and Rosemond Creek just a bit further east. There are campsites, toilets and an information post. Water can be obtained at any of the creeks. Be careful of the bigger rocks when walking on the beach, as they can be very slippery when wet.

Bear Beach to China Beach 9km
Moderate
This last section is considered moderate, but will seem much easier than the last two sections! The trail crosses over Ivanhoe Creek and many other small streams, all of which have good bridges. From here to Mystic Beach is mainly through forest, with a view of the ocean from the cliff top just before reaching Mystic Beach at 2km. There is a campsite here and pit toilets. Note there is no camping at China Beach, so for those who planned an extra day to camp and relax, this would be it. Walk along the beach, and at the eastern edge there is a waterfall going over a sandstone cliff. The trail heads back into the forest and just past 1km crosses a suspension bridge over Pete Wolfe Creek. From here, it's a short walk to China Beach at 0km. China Beach is a fine sand beach with a waterfall at the western end. It's popular for day-use and a good place to picnic, play in the water, watch for whales and build sand castles. A wide gravel trail leads back from the beach through thick, dark mature forest to the two parking areas. For hikers taking the West Coast Trail Express Shuttle, it picks up from the highway, not the parking area, so make sure not to miss it!

Tip
This coastline gets a lot of rain, so expect to encounter rain at any time along the trail. The beginning of the summer (May and June) may be particularly wet and muddy, making the trail more difficult and slow going (in some sections, hikers may find they are only walking 1km an hour). Make sure to allow plenty of time and carry and wear proper equipment (gaiters are highly recommended).

Alternatives
Day-hikes
Having four trailheads, the Juan de Fuca Trail offers plenty of opportunities for some great day-hikes. The Parkinson Creek trailhead gives access to a 10km hike to Botanical Beach or a 9km hike to Sombrio. Botanical Beach offers some short trails (20 minutes each way): Mill Bay, Botany Bay and Botany Loop.

Multi-day Hikes: The West Coast Trail
To add this great trail on at the end and as an alternative is by no means to under-rate it – rather quite the opposite. The West Coast Trail is a strenuous and gruelling seven-day coastal hike in Pacific Rim National Park, beginning or ending just north of Port Renfrew and the Juan de Fuca Trail. Completing the hike requires a great deal of fitness and preparation, a pre-hike orientation and registration. (See 'Pacific Rim National Park' section.)

EAST SOOKE REGIONAL PARK

History
The T'Souke or Coast Salish people used to reef-net salmon around Becher Bay, and in the winter they would collect shellfish, berries and roots at Pedder Bay. After the British had claimed all the land for themselves at the end of the 18th century, Vancouver Island was given to the Hudson Bay Company. By the late 1800s, East Sooke was a very busy place: large sailing ships and dugout canoes ran supplies to and from Victoria, and a steam-powered sawmill provided lumber for the community. In the heart of the present-day park, loggers and miners sought their fortunes: loggers selectively harvested trees up to 3m (9ft) in diameter, and copper and iron were mined for about 100 years at Iron Mine Bay and Mount Macguire. Fishermen were the best off, and from spring to early autumn fish traps were secured in the sea bottom.

Trail 2: East Sooke Coast Trail

Distance:	**10km**
Time:	**6hrs**
Rating:	**moderate–difficult**
Map:	**contact Capital Regional District Parks, tel. (250) 478 3344 or www.crd.bc.ca/parks**
Base:	**Sooke or Victoria**
Best time:	**May–October**

Access

East Sooke Regional Park is 35km west of Victoria (allow an hour to drive from downtown Victoria). Take Highway 14 (Old Island Highway) towards Sooke. Turn left at Gillespie Road and continue down the road. Turn right at East Sooke Road to reach Pike Road, which is the park's most westerly entrance.

Trail Description

From Pike Road, take the trail towards the coast to Iron Mine Bay. The trail passes through a thick forest of Douglas fir, Sitka spruce and western hemlock. The trail to the horseshoe-shaped bay is lush with mosses, ferns and berry shrubs. Going east, the trail passes sharp cliffs where there is a pelagic cormorant roost viewpoint; watch them swoop and dive for food. At Cabin Point, there's a small trap shack that was once used by fishermen. Plants along the trail include Oregon grape, salal and kinnikinnick, which thrive despite the harsh winds and salty spray of the ocean. The trail continues east to along beautiful coastline marked by jagged cliffs to Beechey Head. A little further ahead is Alldridge Point, sacred to the Coast Salish peoples and designated as a provincial heritage point in 1927. Petroglyphs are bruised into the rock – a style particular to this area. Near the end of the trail is Creyke Point, a rocky headland overlooking the ocean. The trail finishes at Aylard Farm, another access point to the park. A heritage apple orchard is a remnant of the last settlement. This is a popular picnic area and its meadows are full of clover, wild rose and blue-eyed grass.

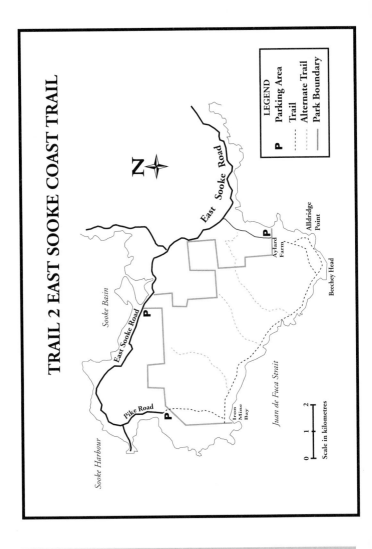

TRAIL 2 EAST SOOKE COAST TRAIL

Look out for deer feeding here at dusk. It's only a five-minute walk to a little beach where you can watch river otters or, at low tide, observe the intertidal life. Be careful of slippery rock ledges on this trail.

Strathcona Park

Natural History

Strathcona Park is located in the centre of Vancouver Island and comprises 250,000 hectares of rugged mountain wilderness. Created in 1911, it is the oldest provincial park in British Columbia and contains the highest point on Vancouver Island, the Golden Hinde, standing at 2200m. At the eastern entrance to Strathcona Park, 40km west of Campbell River, is the eastern frontier of Muchalat territories. The Muchalat lived in many villages along Gold River and Muchalat Inlet and were once warring neighbors of the Mowachaht, 'People of the deer'. Today the two tribes are family. Western red cedar, Douglas fir and western hemlock cover much of the valley and mountain slopes with spectacular wildflower displays during the summer and there is a large deer population as well as Roosevelt elk. Three areas within the park, not accessible by roads and with a total area of more than 122,500 hectares, have been designated nature conservancy areas. Each area has been undisturbed by human activities and contains outstanding examples of natural history and scenery.

Background

In 1899, Joe Drinkwater, a prospector and trapper, discovered Della Falls and named them for his wife. At the turn of the century, he staked claims and built an aerial tramway that still hangs there. Della Falls is the highest free-falling falls in North America, and the sixth highest in the world. It's 440m (1443ft) and drops in three fantastic cascades. The falls drain into a large pond and from there flows over the edge of a cliff.

TRAIL 3: DELLA FALLS TRAIL

Distance:	**36.8km boat ride + 16km hike**
Time:	**3 days (trail – 7hrs one way)**
Rating:	**moderate**
Elevation change:	**350m**
Maps:	**NTS 92F5, 92F6**
Base:	**Port Alberni, Nanaimo, Parksville**
Best time:	**June–September**

Access

Drive west on Highway 4 for about 13km from Port Alberni. Head towards Sproat Lake Provincial Park and then follow the signs for Great Central Lake, Ark Resort and Robertson Creek Hatchery. It's about a 20-minute drive to Ark Resort, where parking is available for a small fee. Those who use their services can park for free. Ark Resort is located at the eastern end of Great Central Lake and provides the best access to the start of the trail. The resort provides a water taxi service, boat rentals, parking and hiking supplies. The water taxi costs $90 per person return trip (Ark Resort to the trailhead) or visitors can rent a canoe or powerboat.

Ark Resort
11,000 Great Central Lake Rd
Site 306, C-1, R.R.#3
Port Alberni, BC
V9Y 7L7
Tel. (250) 723-2657

From here, take a boat up Great Central Lake to the Della Falls trail-head. Great Central Lake is very long (50km), very narrow and very deep (400m), bordered by steep mountains on both sides. With a powerboat, the trip (including hike) is a three-day round-trip. By canoe, it is a six-day trip. Canoe paddlers should leave in the early morning. The north and south shores of this very narrow lake get a lot of rain. By mid-afternoon, the lake is wind-swept by west winds

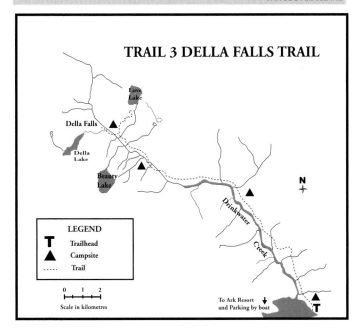

and the water can be very rough with whitecaps. Be on the lookout for standing dead trees on the shore, but follow the shoreline despite the hazards in case of rough water. The western end is marked by flooded standing cedar, fir and spruce.

Trailhead to Della Falls 16km (7hrs)

The trailhead is reached from a wharf. Canoe racks are provided for paddlers to store their canoes as well as pit toilets, designated tent sites and a bear-proof cache. No fires are permitted in the park so a camping stove is necessary. There are no rubbish bins, and all refuse must be packed out. Self-registration envelopes are located at the trailhead and there is a backcountry fee charged per person per night.

Most of the trail follows an old road left over from logging and mining in the early 1900s. Mining equipment can be seen in some parts, remnants that serve as a historical record. The trail leads west following Drinkwater Creek. The first 7km of the trail follows a flat roadbed through mixed second-growth forest. The trail rises in elevation, but swamps in the lower valley mean a lot of bugs. Make sure to bring insect repellent. The trail crosses a bridge at Margaret Creek and then continues through old-growth forest for the next 4km, gently gaining elevation. Some spots on the trail are steep and may slow the pace considerably. Be careful crossing rockslides. At 11km, the trail crosses a new bridge over the gorge at Drinkwater Creek. After the bridge, the trail continues a bit rougher to a bridge at 12.5km. This begins the hardest section. The trail passes through a rockslide that forces hikers close to the creek. The road gains elevation leading to the Love Lake Trail/Mount Septimus junction at 15km. Snow may be present in the higher elevations on the trail – snowmelt is usually finished by late August. The last 1km to Della Falls leads out of the old-growth forest into an avalanche run-out zone to the base of the falls. The roar of the falls can be heard louder and louder. The falls are a series of three successive drops, each about 150m. Snowmelt causes the greatest volume of water over the falls, so the water flow depends on the snow-pack and melt in any given year. The best view of the falls is from the Love Lake Trail, which is a steep switch-backing hike up the opposite side of the valley from the falls. It is possible, but dangerous, to climb to the top of the falls. There is a trail that leads up the left side of the falls that is considered by BC Parks to be a Class 1 hike for experts only. It is very steep and dangerous. A good place to camp is on the north side of Drinkwater Creek about 1km below the falls – the falls are visible from the campsite. Check the map posted for campsites and toilets, and please note that toilet paper is not supplied.

PACIFIC RIM NATIONAL PARK

Natural History

Pacific Rim National Park is divided into three geographic units: the West Coast Trail, the Long Beach Unit and the Broken Islands Group. This vast area of coastal wilderness, known for having some of the heaviest precipitation in the world, is full of rainforests, rocky coast, endless white sand beaches and a huge diversity of flora and fauna. For those who can see only one part of the island, this is arguably the best. Its beauty is magical, spiritual, and the views are extraordinary.

Background

Pacific Rim National Park is 8100 hectares of undisturbed west coast wilderness. The oral histories of the Nuu-chah-nulth claim they have been here since the world was created. Most of what is known of these histories is based on the knowledge of the current elders and observations of others recorded over the past 200 years. A total of 290 native archaeological sites have been identified so far. They represent physical evidence of human involvement in resource extraction: shellfish-processing stations, bark-stripped trees, fish traps and felled trees used in canoe-building. Esowista is the largest of the two Tla-o-qui-aht villages and the only occupied First Nations village inside the boundaries of a Canadian National Park. Formerly known as Clayoquot, Tla-o-qui-aht (pronounced TLA-oo-quee-at) means 'People who are different than they used to be'. Esowista is located at the northern end of Long Beach. A story set at Green Point tells of how a beached whale was cut in half to accommodate the boundary between the Tla-o-qui-aht and 'Long beach people', who have since merged with the Ucluelet First Nation. The name Ucluelet comes from Yo-clutl-Ahts, meaning 'People with good landing places for canoes'. There is also T'ashii, the 'trail' where canoes were portaged from the inland waters at Grice Bay to the open ocean. Just outside the park boundary is Chesterman Beach, called Ch'ahayis by the Nuu-cha-nulth people, meaning 'Sound of ocean on beach'; it is a place where women gathered cedar bark and men trolled for salmon.

At the time of the first European contact, 1778, the population of the area was 9000. There were 23 independent native groups, each holding traditional territories with 21 village sites. Only six of these groups survive today. The people here were rich in comparison to other native groups in North America, and the ocean and forests provided them with food, shelter, clothing and spiritual associations. Western red cedar played an important role: the bark was used to weave clothing, blankets and containers; planks and posts were used to build long houses and dugout canoes. The ocean both provided food and was used for transportation. Salmon, cod and halibut were caught and either eaten immediately or dried for winter. Sea lions, whales and seals were sought for food and also had significant spiritual roles.

After contact with the Europeans, there were significant changes in populations due to epidemics of infectious diseases like smallpox, dysentery and TB. The native people had no defence against these and no knowledge of quarantine. People tried to escape by fleeing to other villages, only to spread the diseases into other populations. The mortality caused by disease and internal warfare in the next 80 years was devastating. Populations on the west coast dropped 75–90%, causing the total disappearance of some groups and the amalgamation of others. Traditionally, groups lived all year round at one village site, but as their territories became enlarged through amalgamation and annexation, new seasonal patterns emerged to take advantage of these acquired resources.

By the late 1800s, with increasing numbers of settlers coming into the area with the fur trade and whaling industries, the native groups took advantage of new economic opportunities such as producing dogfish oil, dried halibut and salmon, and offshore sealing. The tribal centres became closer to the trading centres of the white settlers, and the natives started to supplement their diets with foods from the trading posts like flour and sugar, which replaced their traditional dependence on local food sources. More settlers were attracted by coast forest and fishing resources, and a prosperous export lumber trade developed. The salmon fishery became the most valuable fishery on the west coast.

This part of the west coast has been dubbed the 'Graveyard of the Pacific' because since 1803 240 ships have become shipwrecked along the treacherous coast. A lighthouse was built at Cape Brule in 1874 and in 1890; the West Coast Telegraph was completed between Victoria and Cape Beale and a second lighthouse built at Carmanah Point. The year 1906 saw the tragic wreck of the passenger steamer *Valencia*, with 126 lives lost. The telegraph line became the Lifesaving Trail, and a third lighthouse was built at Pachena Point near the site of the wreck. Because of high costs, the Lifesaving Trail was only cleared from Bamfield to Carmanah Point, and beyond this the rest of the trail remained the original primitive telegraph line. As shipwrecks were a frequent occurrence, the trail helped to save many lives. By the 1940s, more sophisticated navigation equipment had

been developed and trail maintenance was discontinued. It was rede-
veloped by Parks Canada in the 1970s and is today known as the
West Coast Trail, one of North America's best-known and most challenging hikes.

During World War II, a large airfield was built on land surrounded
by the Long Beach Unit of the park, and a road was built to connect
the communities of Tofino and Ucluelet. Highway 4 was built in
1959, connecting Long Beach to the rest of the world.

Tofino and Ucluelet Accomodation

Whalers On The Port Guesthouse
81 West Street
PO Box 296
Tofino, BC V0R 2Z0
Tel. (250) 725-3443
Fax (250) 725-3463
Email: info@tofinohostel.com

Located in downtown Tofino, with breathtaking views of Clayoquot
Sound, this hostel offers a shuttle bus to Long Beach and Ucluelet
and rents out surfboards and kayaks along with lots of other perks.

Pacific Rim Resort and Campground
1451 Pacfic Rim Highway
Tofino, BC
Tel. (250) 725-3202
Mussel Beach Wilderness Campground
Clayoquot District, BC

Directions: From Tofino/Ucluelet Highway junction (Junction 4), it's a
20-minute drive – 5km of paved road, 8km of logging roads. Follow
the signs to Mussel Beach. Turn on Albion Rd and take the gravel
road to Vet and Mussel Beach.

Ucluelet Campground
260 Sea Plane Base
Ucluelet, BC

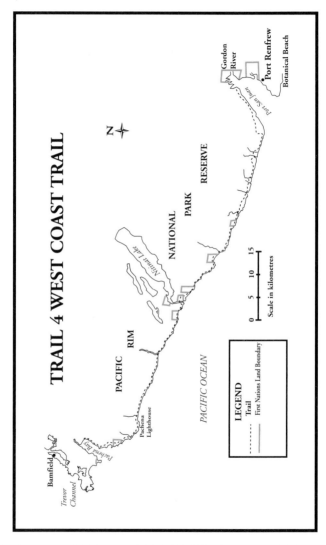

TRAIL 4 WEST COAST TRAIL

N

PACIFIC

RIM

NATIONAL

PARK

RESERVE

Nitinat Lake

Bamfield

Trevor Channel

Pachena Bay

Pachena
Lighthouse

PACIFIC OCEAN

Gordon
River

Port Renfrew

Botanical Beach

Port San Juan

LEGEND

Trail

First Nations Land Boundary

0   5   10   15

Scale in kilometres

WEST COAST TRAIL UNIT

TRAIL 4: THE WEST COAST TRAIL

Distance:	75km
Time:	6–8 days
Rating:	difficult
Base:	Port Renfrew or Victoria
Best time:	open May 1–Sept 30

Tide tables needed and trail use registration mandatory

Access

The West Coast Trail isn't reached from Tofino but rather from the south coast – Victoria and Port Renfrew or from Port Alberni (depending on which trailhead you start from). The Gordon River trailhead is located 5km north of Port Renfrew, 2 hours from Victoria on Highway 14. The Pachena Bay trailhead is 5km south of Bamfield. It is a drive of 1hr 30mins on gravel logging roads from Port Alberni. The West Coast Trail Express Shuttle Bus (tel. (250) 477-8774) leaves daily from both Nanaimo and Victoria.

Background

The West Coast Trail is an internationally renowned, challenging and rugged 75km hike from Pachena Bay to Gordon River. It is for experienced and physically fit hikers, and demands both stamina and proficiency in backcountry wilderness and camping skills. It cannot be overemphasized that this hike is not for novices, and accidents and injuries are common. Hikers must be completely self-sufficient and be prepared for long days, heavy packs, slippery, difficult terrain and bad weather. Early in the season, it is not unknown for the trail to be waist-deep with mud in some places. In 1992, a quota system was put in place to prevent overcrowding and to reduce environmental degradation. Each day between May 1 and September 30, 26 hikers are allowed to start at each end of the trail. This includes 20 reserved spaces and 6 wait-list spaces (first-come-first-served). The trail is closed for the rest of the year due to extremely dangerous conditions.

A Trail Use Permit is mandatory for anyone remaining overnight in this unit of the park. Permits can be obtained from the Park Information/Registration Centres near the two trailheads. Note that there are no banking or cash advance facilities in the villages of Bamfield or Port Renfrew, or at the Park Information/Registration Centres. Trail Use Permits will not be issued to children under the age of six.

Pachena Bay Information/Registration Centre
Tel/Fax (250) 728-3234
Open daily 9am–5pm, 1 May to 5 October

Gordon River Information/Registration Centre
Tel (250) 647-5434
Fax (250) 647-0016
Open daily 9am–5pm, 1 May to 5 October

Pacific Rim National Park Reserve
Park Administration Office
Tel (250) 726-7721
Open all year

There are also two major water crossings along the trail, and ferry fees are payable upon registration. Spaces may be reserved up to three months in advance or prospective hikers can show up as any unused quota spaces, cancellations or no-show reservations will be allotted to hikers by the wait-list system. During peak season – July to mid-September – hikers may wait from 1 to 3 days using the wait-list system.

Before being issued with a Trail Use Permit, visitors must attend a one-hour orientation session, pay the trail fee and the ferry fees, and register on the trail. Orientation sessions begin at 9.30am; noon, 1.30pm and 3.30pm. Total fees are around $125, including the registration fee, which includes the Hiker Preparation Guide and West Coast Trail Map. The Hiker Preparation Guide, which changes annually, can also be found online at: www.sookenet.com/activity/trails/wctguide.html.

Alternatives
- Day-hikers are permitted in the West Coast Trail Unit of the park but must obtain a free Day Use Permit before hiking. These can be obtained from the park information/registration centres or the Park Administration Office at 2185 Ocean Terrace Road, Ucluelet (tel. (250) 726-7721). Day-hikers starting at Gordon River will have to pay for return ferry service across Gordon River (about $15 per person).
- The Quu'as West Coast Trail Society is a partnership between Parks Canada and three First Nations: Pacheedaht, Ditidaht and Huu-Ay-Aht. To experience the West Coast Trail through the eyes, hearts and histories of the First Nations, a rare experience only available through the First Nations people in their communities, contact:

Quu'as West Coast Trail Society

PO Box 253

Port Alberni, BC

V9H 7M7

Tel. (250) 723-4393

Email: qwct@cedar.alberni.net

Website: http:/cedar.alberni.net/quuas/

LONG BEACH UNIT

The Long Beach Unit is the most accessible of the three park units. It is located on a broad coastal plain just northwest of Barkley Sound, a large inlet of the Pacific Ocean, near the communities of Tofino and Ucluelet. This area is most famous for long sandy beaches. Long Beach and Schooner Cove stretch out over 16km, with the beach at Florencia Bay to the south adding another 6.4km to its span. In January 2000, Clayoquot Sound was designated as an international biosphere reserve. The Long Beach area makes up a core area of this reserve, protecting its long sand beaches among other significant ecosystems.

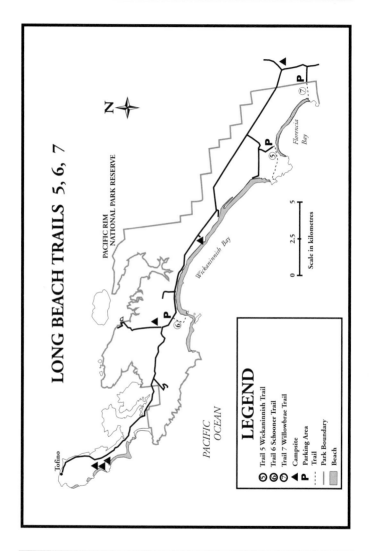

LONG BEACH TRAILS 5, 6, 7

PACIFIC RIM
NATIONAL PARK RESERVE

Florencia Bay

Wickaninnish Bay

PACIFIC OCEAN

Tofino

N

Scale in kilometres
0   2.5   5

LEGEND

5 Trail 5 Wickaninnish Trail
6 Trail 6 Schooner Trail
7 Trail 7 Willowbrae Trail
▲ Campsite
P Parking Area
----- Trail
Park Boundary
Beach

Access

The Long Beach Unit is located between the coastal communities of Tofino and Ucluelet on Vancouver Island's west coast. From Port Alberni, follow Highway 4 west. It's about a 90-minute drive, 108km, on a steep and winding road. At the Tofino/Ucluelet junction, turn right to reach the southern boundary of the park. There is an entry fee, as this is a national park. Most national parks charge a fee and the money goes back into the same park, so visitors are directly investing into the future of the park they are visiting. There are nine short hiking trails in the Long Beach Unit – these are the three longest.

TRAIL 5: WICKANINNISH TRAIL

Distance:	**5km return**
Rating:	**easy**

This trail goes along Quisitis Point and links Long Beach to Florencia (Wreck) Bay. From the Wickaninnish Centre, first take the South Beach Trail. This winds through a forest of wind-pruned Sitka spruce that fringes the shoreline. Short little side-trails lead to coves of sand or cobble that are enclosed by headlands. One of these coves is lined with a cobble beach called Lismer Beach. At the far end of the beach, a boardwalk ascends over the headland towards South Beach. The trail is lined with walls of salal and salmonberry, and there are great views of Lismer Beach and Wickaninnish Beach. At the top of the hill, take the trail to the left – the Wickaninnish Trail to Florencia Bay. Wickaninnish Bay was named for an influential and powerful Nuu-chah-nulth chief and leader of the Clayoquot people in the 1800s. This trail is a remnant of the early overland route that connected Tofino and Ucluelet. About halfway along, the old corduroy log surface is visible between a colourful mat of sphagnum peat mosses. Tiny clusters of green leaves covered with tiny red droplets can be seen in the carpet. This plant is called the sundew and it attracts insects to its tiny leaves and then digests the entangled victims. The trail ends at a parking area near a good viewpoint.

TRAIL 6: SCHOONER TRAIL

Distance:	**2.1km return**
Rating:	**easy**

This trail starts at the parking area 4.8km north of the Green Point Campground on Highway 4. The trail winds through a cedar-hemlock forest and bridges a small salmon-spawning stream. There are stairs that descend down to the beach. During the descent, the cedar-hemlock forest changes to Sitka spruce. Sitka spruce is well adapted to the coastal environment. Exposure to wind, salt and sand kills most young trees, but the Sitka spruce seedlings thrive on the magnesium-rich soil and form what is called the Sitka spruce fringe. This fringe skirts the entire outer coast of Vancouver Island, as well as the Queen Charlotte Islands and exposed coastal sections of mainland BC.

TRAIL 7: WILLOWBRAE TRAIL

Distance:	**2.8km return**
Rating:	**easy**

There is no sign showing access to this trail from the highway. The Willowbrae Road intersects Highway 4 2km south of the Tofino/ Ucluelet/Port Alberni junction. There is a small parking area on the gravel road just opposite Willowbrae Road. This trail retraces the steps of the many people who used it as a link between their homes and the villages of Tofino and Ucluelet. Before the road was built to join the two communities in 1942, it was common practice to carry all groceries and supplies from here to Tofino, traversing difficult terrain and a 16km stretch of sandy beach! Part of the trail was once surfaced with slabs of cedar, hand-cut and laid across in a corduroy pattern. The trail was once wide enough for a horse-drawn wagon, but now salal and deer fern have grown over it making it narrower. Most of the remaining corduroy is overgrown with sphagnum moss. The trail approaches the shore, where the roar of the surf can be heard. There's a small bridge and then the trail divides. To the left is the Half Moon Bay Trail. Continue straight ahead, descend a steep hill and emerge from the forest at the southeast end of Florencia Bay, an open and often misty beach.

Alternatives

A fantastic side-trip from Tofino is to Hot Springs Cove. Hot Springs Cove is one of the most magnificent hot springs in the world, still in its natural state and without crowds – in fact the solitary experience is quite likely, especially off-season or early in the morning. It is located in Macquinna Provincial Park in the remote northern end of Clayoquot Sound and can be reached via boat (water taxi) from Tofino or floatplane. Make sure to make arrangements to be picked up later in the day or the next day – camping overnight is highly recommended. From the dock, it is a short, easy hike into the magical hot springs. Hot Springs Cove has three rock-lined pools tiered down a slope with the last pool spilling into the ocean below. A waterfall splashes into the pool at one end. At high tide, the lowest pool disappears into the ocean. A hot mineral steam bath that rejuvenates the soul in the surroundings of old-growth rainforest on the edge of the world. Swim-suits are optional.

FLORES ISLAND

'We are only a small part of, but certainly not in control of, Mother Nature.' – Chief Louis Frank, Ahousaht

'Old growth forests are all we have left. It is a legacy for the generation of young people. We should treat it as our forefathers practiced, in First Nations' spirituality.' – Chief Earl Maquinna George

Background

The Ahousaht, 'People facing away from the ocean', are the largest Nuu-chah-nulth community. They were whalers and, until 150 years ago, lived on the smaller island of Vargas to the south. It was the

Otsosaht who lived on Flores Island; they gave the Ahousaht their whaling ceremonies and possessed salmon-bearing rivers that the Ahousaht coveted. The Ahousaht won these rivers after a long war in the 1800s; these battles were fought on the beaches of Flores, Vargas and Bartlett, and included most peoples on Clayoquot Sound. Not many of the Otsosaht survived. Stories tell that the great Ahousaht war chief, Qamiina, prepared for war by practising ritual diving in an underwater cave. He is said to have bitten a piece of fin off a basking shark. In 1993, several Ahousaht women formed Walk the Wild Side, a non-profit First Nations women's ecotourism initiative to help secure steady jobs and income for their community. The Ahousaht Wild Side Heritage Trail was built in the spring of 1996 with a grant from Youth Services Canada, WCWC and Ahousaht First Nations. The aim was to train 20 youth in ecotourism and clear an ancient trail to the outside beaches on Flores Island. The project continued into 1997 and received additional support. Ahousaht, a First Nations village, is the gateway to the trail. The trail traverses a dozen surf-swept sandy beaches and rainforested headlands, and winds its way to the top of Flores Mountain, the highest point on the island at 970m.

The Nuu-chah-nulth people are guided by a philosophy that they call Hishuk-ish ts'awalk, meaning 'everything is one'. It recognizes that communities, cultures, economies and environments are interwoven and impact on one another.

On January 21st 2000, Clayoquot Sound was designated as a UNESCO biosphere reserve. It covers an area of 3500km^2 and encompasses a whole range of ecosystems, including lakes, rivers and streams, large areas of unlogged temperate rainforests, alpine peaks, inshore marine areas, mudflats, estuaries, rocky coastal shores and long sandy beaches. Core areas include the Long Beach Unit of Pacific Rim National Park and over 95,000 hectares of provincial park. The reserve designation acknowledges aboriginal title and rights and doesn't prejudice ongoing treaty negotiations.

Getting There

The *Spirit of Marktosis* seabus from Tofino to Flores Island leaves daily at 10.30am and 4.00pm and takes about 45 minutes. The cost is $12. Water taxis also travel back and forth at various times in the day. The seabus is located at the First Street dock in Tofino. The boat trip alone is fascinating as it passes through reefs, islands and inlets into the heart of Clayoquot Sound.

Flores Island Accommodation
Hummingbird International Hostel
General Delivery
Ahousaht, BC
V0R 1A0
Tel/Fax (250) 670-9679
Email: mvblaze@home.com

TRAIL 8: THE AHOUSAHT WILD SIDE HERITAGE TRAIL

Distance:	16km
Time:	overnight
Rating:	moderate
Maps:	NTS 92E/8
Base:	Tofino
Best time:	May–September

Tide tables needed

This trail was used by many generations of the Nuu-chah-nulth peoples and links up the native village of Ahousaht on the southeast side with a dozen sandy beaches and rainforested headlands on the wild western side. It starts at Marktosis and goes through Gibson Marine Park to Cow Bay, through First Nations reserve land. It then continues 4km up the summit of Mount Flores (902m). The trail traverses near the summer feeding bays of the grey whale and through the forested habitats of many bird and wildlife species. Both the Ahousaht Village trailhead and the Cow Bay trailhead are accessible by water taxi from Tofino. The trail is a combination of boardwalks, beach and rough forest. The trail is rugged and can be very wet after heavy rains, and the boardwalks can be slippery. Bring plenty of water as it is difficult to obtain along the trail, particularly in late summer.

Guided Options
Walk the Wild Side
General Delivery
Ahousaht, BC
V0R 1A0
Tel. 1-888-670-9586

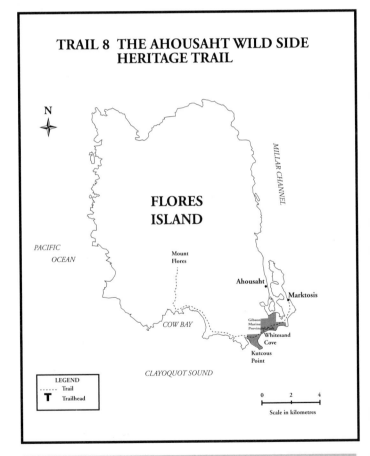

TRAIL 8 THE AHOUSAHT WILD SIDE HERITAGE TRAIL

N

MILLAR CHANNEL

FLORES ISLAND

PACIFIC OCEAN

Mount Flores

Ahousaht

Marktosis

Gibson Marine Provincial Park

COW BAY

Whitesand Cove

Kutcous Point

CLAYOQUOT SOUND

LEGEND	
- - - - -	Trail
T	Trailhead

0   2   4

Scale in kilometres

Cape Scott Provincial Park

Background

This area is a rugged coastal wilderness with heavy rainstorms and violent winds. The Nahwitti people believed the great wind came from the anus of Malalanukw. The storms prevented them from fishing and gathering food, and they were slowly starving to death. They called upon their supernatural chief to defeat Malalanukw. The chief set him on fire and made him promise that every so often there would be four days in a row of good weather so his people could harvest their food. In the beginning, the Tlatlasikwala, Nakumgilisala and Yutlinuk shared the Cape Scott area. The Yutlinuk of the Scott Islands died out in the 1800s, and the other two groups joined together and moved to Hope Island in the mid-1850s. They lived there until 1954 and then, with a population of just 32, joined the Koskimo and moved to Quatsino Sound. Today they are known collectively as the Nahwitti and have six reserves; two of them are within the park boundaries. Two settlement attempts were made by Danish pioneers in 1897 and again in 1910. After several years of hardship because of adverse weather and lack of access to markets, they were forced to give up and leave. Little remains of these days except for names like Nels Bight and Frederiksen Point and some fragile buildings. A small radar station was built at Cape Scott in 1942 during World War II for purposes of national security. It remained in operation until 1945, spotting only a flock of geese during this period.

Natural History

Cape Scott is a natural gathering spot for migratory birds: waterfowl, sandhill cranes, trumpeter swans, pelagic cormorants, snipes, sandpipers and plovers. Waterfowl and geese are especially common at Hansen Lagoon, with gulls and seabirds gathering along the shore near the cape. Seals, otters and sea lions inhabit the offshore island. The upland areas are forested with red and yellow cedar, lodgepole pine, hemlock and fir, and the undergrowth is mainly salal, salmonberry, evergreen huckleberry and fern. The forested and open upland areas support populations of deer, elk, bear and wolves.

Port Hardy Accommodation

Port Hardy is the largest community on northern Vancouver Island with a population of about 5000. There are many B&Bs and hotels in Port Hardy, and the Port Hardy and District Chamber of Commerce operates a reservation service which will phone around for accommodation to save the visitor time and money (tel. (250) 949-7622 or email: phcc@island.net). It is highly recommended that any accommodation needed during busy summer months be reserved well in advance. Port Hardy is a busy port, with the Discovery Coast and Inside Passage ferries, and if left to the last minute it is highly likely that all the B&Bs, in particular, will be full. Check out the museum in Port Hardy prior to hiking the Cape Scott Trail to learn more about the cultural history of the area.

TRAIL 9: CAPE SCOTT TRAIL

Distance:	**23.6km (one way)**
Time:	**8hrs (one way)**
Rating:	**moderate–difficult**
Maps:	**NTS 102 1/9 and 1/16**
Base:	**Port Hardy, Holberg**
Best time:	**July–August**

Tide tables needed

Access

The only access to Cape Scott Provincial Park is the trails. From Port Hardy, it's a 67km drive on a combination of highways and private logging roads. Port Hardy is at the northern terminus of Highway 19, which connects the northern communities to the south of the island. There is a parking area at the Cape Scott and San Josef Bay trailhead near the southeast corner of the park. The parking is on Western Forest Products land and is provided by the company for park users. Be careful driving on the logging roads and keep your headlights on at all times.

Yoho National Park

Emerald Lake in Yoho National Park

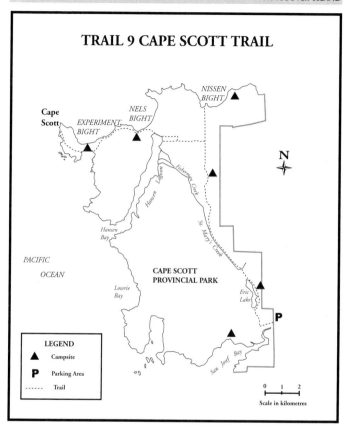

TRAIL 9 CAPE SCOTT TRAIL

NISSEN
BIGHT ▲

Cape
Scott

NELS
BIGHT

EXPERIMENT
BIGHT

▲

▲

Hansen Lagoon

Fisherman Creek

N

▲

Hansen
Bay

St. Mary's Creek

PACIFIC

OCEAN

CAPE SCOTT
PROVINCIAL PARK

Lowrie
Bay

Eric
Lake

▲

P

▲

San Josef Bay

LEGEND

▲   Campsite

P   Parking Area

·····   Trail

0   1   2

Scale in kilometres

Trail Description

From the parking area, it is an 8- to 10-hour hike to Cape Scott. After
1–2km (about an hour), the trail reaches Eric Lake, a basin full of cut-
throat trout. There's an old wharf near the campsite. It's about two
more hours to Fisherman River Bridge, where the trail leaves the rainforest and heads into lowlands and bog. There are bridges and boardwalks built all along the trail to protect the vegetation. Approaching

the cape, the trail branches at the head of Hansen Lagoon. Hansen Lagoon is a stopping place for Canada geese and other waterfowl on the Pacific Flyway. This is the Nissen Bight cut-off. The left branch leads to Nels Bight, the Cape Scott lighthouse and the west coast, and the right branch goes to the northern cape and Nissen Bight. From the Fisherman River Bridge to Nissen Bight is 3.7km and takes between 2hrs and 2hrs 30mins to reach the rocky shoreline. There's a campsite there as well. The trail leading west to Cape Scott passes through the old community and comes out at Hansen Lagoon. At the lagoon, hikers can head to Fisherman River where it enters Hansen Lagoon. By turning right at the lagoon signpost, the route reaches Nels Bight, a 2km stretch of beach. Starting at the west end of Nels Bight, the trail to Cape Scott is 16km return. The trail that leads to Experiment Bight, Guise Bay and Cape Scott follows an old jeep road that originated in World War II when the radar station operated. The sand neck is so narrow here that, from the height of the land, both sides of Vancouver Island, east and west, can be seen. From Guise Bay there is a plank road that leads up to the lighthouse. At the very tip of the island, there's a view of the jagged landscape, the Scott Channel and the Scott Islands. The Cape Scott Lighthouse watches over the treacherous, rocky west coast where huge breakers crash against the rocks.

Alternatives
A good one-day hike is to San Josef Bay, 2.5km one way. Most back-packers set up camp on the sandy beach fronted by sea stacks.

HAIDA GWAII – THE QUEEN CHARLOTTE ISLANDS

In Haida it is said, 'Ginn 7waadluwaan gud7ahl Kwaagiidang'*
– everything depends on everything else.

'Our culture, our heritage is the child of respect and intimacy
with the land and sea. Like the forests, the roots of our people
are intertwined such that that the greatest troubles cannot
overcome us...' – from the Haida Constitution

Natural History

The Haida, who have lived here for 10,000 years, call these islands
Haida Gwaii or 'Islands of the people'. Haida Gwaii is made up of
about 150 islands, the tops of a submerged ridge, located between
50 and 130km from mainland. The two main islands are Graham in
the north and Moresby in the south, and the population is about 6000
scattered between several communities, including the two main
Haida communities, Skidegate and Old Massett. Scientists believe
that portions of Haida Gwaii escaped glaciation in the last ice age
and that these areas provided a refuge for plants and animals in which
they survived and evolved. Haida Gwaii has an international reputation as the Canadian Galapagos – a showcase of evolution. Species
and subspecies, including the pine marten, ermine, Saw-whet owl
and the world's largest black bear – have evolved here slightly differ-
ently from anywhere else in the world. Haida Gwaii has several
protected areas, internationally recognized as environmental jewels:
Naikoon Provincial Park, Duu Guusd Tribal Park, Delkatla Wildlife
Sanctuary, Gwaii Haanas National Park Reserve/Haida Heritage Site
and Sgaang Gwaay (UNESCO world heritage site).

These areas have all been recognized after hard-won battles. In
1985, a combination of Haida and environmentalists blockaded a

---

* 7 is used to represent a glottal stop in many of the native languages.

logging road on Lyell Island, today part of Gwaii Haanas. In 1996, the Haida and Greenpeace protested against the destruction of Haida Gwaii's temperate rainforests – the logging company was using one of the world's largest log barges that can hold the equivalent of the load carried by 400 logging trucks. These forests were disappearing before the people's very eyes. Today, with coalitions like Forest Renewal BC and Fisheries Renewal BC, local groups are able to begin reclaiming their resources with projects including salmon habitat restoration and stock enhancement and community trail efforts like the Spirit Lake Trail. Visitors to Haida Gwaii can continue to be enticed by rugged coastline, remote wilderness, endless sandy beaches, the relationship its people have with their environment and the diversity of life found here including grey whales, orcas, sea lions and bald eagles.

Background

According to Haida legend, Haida Gwaii is the place where time began. To the Haida, their world is like the edge of a knife cutting between the depths of the sea, which to them symbolizes the underworld, and the forested mountains, which mark the transition to the upper world. On one side of the knife is the past, and on the other the future – the key being to live on that edge, which marks the present. The Haida believe in the sky world, the earth and the underworld, and that it is vital to maintain harmony between these zones. Disharmony in any one is reflected in an unfortunate event in the human world, such as a storm, a landslide or failure of a fish run. The Haida are a canoe people and have strong connections to the sea. Their villages were always on the coast, with the water being their major transportation route. Their canoes allowed them to travel long distances, hunt sea mammals and fish offshore. The Haida canoe played a fundamental role in Haida tradition and history; they were the primary modes of transport for both marriages and wars. All neighbouring First Nations recognized the skill of Haida canoe makers and the quality of their canoes. They ranged in length from 30 to 70ft and were a major trade item, being prized as **the** superior ocean-going craft. Haida canoes are carved from red cedar, steamed into classical form and the hull is painted black, while the bow and stern are elaborately painted with representations of supernatural creatures. These traditions continue today.

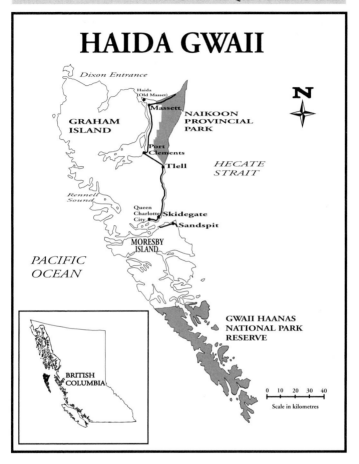

Before the Europeans arrived, estimates of the Haida population on Haida Gwaii range from 10,000 to 30,000. In 1774, at the time of first contact with the Europeans, there were at least 50 thriving villages. Contact with the Europeans, who brought TB and smallpox, nearly annihilated the Haida and whole lineages were lost. In 1787, Captain

George Dixon named Haida Gwaii the Queen Charlotte Islands after his ship and also after the wife of King George III. Between 1790 and 1860, major epidemics of smallpox struck three times. Some 95% of the population was wiped out, and by 1915 the Haida population reached its lowest of only 588 people; Massett and Skidegate were the only permanent villages to survive the 19th century. In 1877, missionaries arrived with the aim of transforming 'primitive' people into 'civilized' people. In doing so, they disregarded a way of life that had been established for centuries. The Haida songs, dances and ceremonies were a threat to the missionary way of thinking. Their totem poles were chopped down, left to rot, used for firewood or sold, and the Haida were told not carve them any more because it was a heathen act. In 1880, the Canadian government made an amendment to the Indian Act making it a criminal offence to participate in the potlatch, the most important Haida ceremony. To further weaken their spirit, the children were taken away by the government and sent to residential schools far from their homes. They were forbidden to speak the Haida language and punished if they did so. They were robbed of their beliefs, self-esteem and self-worth. In many cases, they were not allowed to visit their families and homes for years and returned as strangers. This occurred as recently as the 1960s.

The Haida not only survived but have also adapted and carried their cultural heritage into mainstream 21st-century society. Hunting and gathering, feasting and ceremonies are still a part of everyday life, along with a mix of modern careers and lifestyles. The Haida are in a process of reclaiming the things they've lost. There are more Haida artefacts in museums than in all of Haida Gwaii. The Haida are trying to get back these things: art pieces, totem poles, even remains of their ancestors whose graves were dug up and lie in boxes in museum warehouses. The Haida are reclaiming their language after government attempts to assimilate them into western culture through residential schools. The Haida language is an isolate – it is not related to any other language. The Haida spoke different dialects depending on which clan they came from. In the past, it did not have a written form, and stories and traditions were passed on orally or represented visually in their artwork. In 1998, the Skidegate Haida Immersion Program was established to ensure the future of the Haida language. The elders, who speak different dialects, came together to agree on one way of speaking so that it can be taught to and spoken by the younger generations. Today, Haida Language and Haida Studies add an important element to the education system. There has been a resurgence of Haida culture and artistic traditions including celebrations at potlatches. At a potlatch, large numbers of guests (sometimes a thousand or more) are invited by the host to commemorate a significant occasion. This could be the passing on of a chief's title or property, a marriage or a memorial to honour someone who has died. By honouring their invitations, guests validate the claims and actions of the host and they are compensated with feasting and gifts. Haida Gwaii has one of the highest concentrations of artists in North America, and many of them are among the best in the world with designs in cedar, gold, silver and argillite, a soft black slate found only on Haida Gwaii and only available to Haida artists. The Haida have their own constitution and their own flag in defence of their sovereignty.

Note on Haida Totem Poles

> **'Since, in the past, the totem pole was the only formal visual document, I cannot overstate its importance in our development as a nation'** – Robert Davidson, from *Eagle Transforming: The Art of Robert Davidson*

The totem pole is a declaration or document that displays images that are the family crests or that represent important events of a family, a village or history of the people. It displays the wealth of a clan and its accomplishments and lays claim to the crests it displays. Sometimes a pole will illustrate a story. Traditionally, when a new chief took his position, he was obligated to raise a pole in honour of the deceased chief whose position he was filling. Red cedar is traditionally used for the poles because of the height and size it grows to, and because it has a nice straight grain and is easy to carve. Red cedar also weathers well, as it has a natural preservative that helps prevent rotting. Dry rot in the centre is not a problem, because the Haida make the pole by cutting off about a third of the back and hollowing it out. Hollowing makes the pole lighter, so it can be raised more easily, and also slows down the cracking as the wood dries out. Haida carvers and artists are renowned for their sense of balance and symmetry. In June 2001, six new poles were raised at the Qay'llnagaay Heritage Centre in Skidegate, the first six of a total of 14 to be raised there.

Getting There

Getting to Haida Gwaii is an adventure in itself. Air Canada flies daily into Sandspit on Moresby Island from Vancouver (www.aircanada.ca or call 1-888-247-2262 for flight schedules and fares). Flights from Vancouver itself can be expensive, but if Haida Gwaii is your primary destination, tickets from Europe to Sandspit do not usually cost much more than those from Vancouver to Sandspit! There are also daily flights from Prince Rupert on Harbour Air (tel. 1-800-689-4234). However, the most common and more scenic option is with BC Ferries. The ferry sails six times a week during the summer from Prince Rupert to Skidegate Landing on Graham Island. The daytime trips take about 6 hours, with the overnight sailings being slightly longer. The scenery is breathtaking, and whales and porpoises are often spotted along the way. Prince Rupert is a harbour city in northern BC and is well positioned for business pursuits in the Pacific Rim. It is also the Canadian gateway to Alaska. The land route from Vancouver to Prince Rupert is via inland Prince George and is long. For this reason and many others, getting to Prince Rupert via the Inside Passage ferry from northern Vancouver Island is the exciting, not-to-be-missed option. The Inside Passage route is from Port Hardy to Prince Rupert and takes 15 hours. This cruise is a trip in itself: it travels through calm inlets and open sections of ocean, and passes island upon island, majestic mountains and forest with often sightings of eagles, whales and dolphins. Some of the Inside Passage sailings and Queen Charlotte sailings connect; contact BC Ferries for more information: tel. 1-888-223-3779 (within BC) or (250) 386-3431 or www.bcferries.com – full schedules and fares online. Vehicle reservations are strongly recommended at all times.

Getting Around

BC Ferries accepts just about any vehicle on board, but it is possible to arrive in Haida Gwaii on your own two feet and still manage to get around. The Airport Shuttle (tel. 1-877-747-4461) meets all Air Canada flights into Sandspit. Eagle Cabs Ltd operates both the Airport Shuttle and Island Transit, a bus service connecting Masset and Sandspit with all places in between. Call (250) 559-4461 or 1-877-747-4461 for schedules and fares. Reservations are recommended for both. It is possible to rent a car and petrol is available in all towns.

A couple of good options are: Rustic Rentals in Queen Charlotte City, tel. 1-877-559-4641, fax (250) 559-4557, email citires@qcislands. net (they have cars, trucks, sport vehicles and campers for hire and offer ferry pick-up and delivery); and Budget, which has offices at the airport, in Sandspit, Queen Charlotte City and Masset (tel. 1-800-577-3228 or (250) 637-5688). Driving around Haida Gwaii is easy: the paved Yellowhead Highway (Highway 16) connects all of the communities on Graham Island. A 20-minute ferry crossing between Skidegate Landing and Alliford Bay connects Graham and Moresby Islands. There are 12 sailings a day in each direction. Bicycles can be rented from Moresby Island Guest House in Sandspit (tel. (250) 637-5300) or Premier Creek Lodging in Queen Charlotte City (tel. 1-888-322-3388). Although not recommended in other parts of BC, failing those options many locals get around easily and safely by hitchhiking.

Driving Distances

Skidegate to Queen Charlotte City	7km
Skidegate to Tlell	40km
Skidegate to Masset	101km
Queen Charlotte to Sandspit	22km

Climate

The climate of Haida Gwaii is moderated by the maritime influence and it is generally mild with no extremes in temperature. Precipitation is almost always in the form of rain, although there is some snow in winter. The wettest months are October to January, although there can still be a fair amount of rain in the summer as well. In any month the weather can be unpredictable, with sun, wind, fog and rain all within a few hours. Average temperatures in summer are 15–20°C, and in winter 0–8°C. From May to July, Haida Gwaii enjoys 18–20 hours of daylight.

Accommodation

Haida Gwaii has many B&Bs, guesthouses, hotels and motels. Below are just a couple of suggestions. There is also plenty of camping around; some are mentioned with the trails.

Tlell
Cacilia's B&B
Box 3, Tlell
V0T 1Y0
Tel./Fax (250) 557-4664
Email: ceebysea@qcislands.net
This rustic log house nestled in the dunes is a two-minute walk from a secluded sandy beach. Cacilia is a perfect host and cook, and her driftwood swings in the kitchen and other small touches around the house make this a perfect base while discovering this magical place. She also has tent sites.

Queen Charlotte City
Premier Creek Hostel & Lodging
Box 268, Queen Charlotte City
Tel. (250) 559-8415/1-888-322-3388
Fax (250) 559-8198
Email: Premier@qcislands.net

Dorothy & Mike's Guest House
Box 595
3125- 2nd Ave, Queen Charlotte City
BC, V0T 1S0
Tel. (250) 559-8439

Masset
Rapid Ritchie's Rustic Rentals
Rich Shultz & Toni Smith
Box 667, #13 Tow Hill Rd
Tel./Fax (250) 626-5472
www.beachcabins.com

Jean's Beach House Lodging B&B
Box 147, Masset
V0T 1M0
Tel. (250) 626-5662/1-888-273-4444
Email: jeansbh@island.net

TRAIL 10: SPIRIT LAKE TRAIL

Distance:	**3km (circular)**
Time:	**1hr 30mins – 2hrs return**
Rating:	**easy–moderate**
Base:	**Skidegate**
Best time:	**year round**

The Haida people have long used the Spirit Lake area for harvesting cedar and other plants, and the area features in many stories and legends. The most famous is the legend of the Wasco sea monster. Spirits have always existed around the lakes, and the Wasco sea monster was a spirit undefined in shape and feared by all. The story is about a brave hunter who put the spirit to rest, making the Spirit Lake area safe again for the people.

Access
The trailhead is located off Highway 16 in Skidegate across from the George Brown Recreation Hall, and is marked with a stunning carved cedar gateway designed by carver Pat Wesley as a memorial to the Spirit Lake Wasco (sea wolf). Lead carvers were Bill Bellis and Pat Wesley, who spent 10 weeks on the carving before it was erected in the summer of 2000.

Trail Description
This is a well-marked gravel trail that winds through alders, ferns and cedars. Watch out for devil's club, which grows on both sides of the trail. Its spines are almost impossible to dislodge. The Haida used devil's club for medicinal purposes, and the spines were used as hooks to catch black cod and octopus. There are boardwalk bridges to cross the creeks. This is a good trail on which to see culturally modified trees (CMTs). These are trees from which large strips of cedar have been removed. The Haida use cedar bark for weaving hats, baskets, roses, headbands and clothing.

The trail climbs through second-growth then old-growth forest before reaching a junction. Turning right here leads to the Spirit Lake

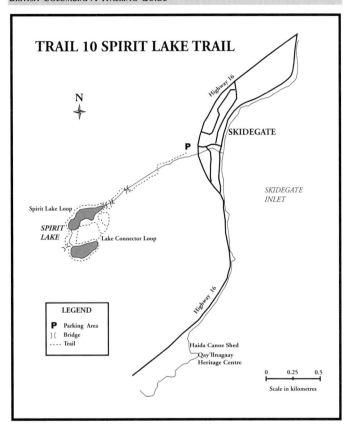

TRAIL 10 SPIRIT LAKE TRAIL

N

Highway 16

SKIDEGATE

P

*SKIDEGATE
INLET*

Spirit Lake Loop

*SPIRIT
LAKE*

Lake Connector Loop

LEGEND

P Parking Area
)(Bridge
- - - - Trail

Highway 16

Haida Canoe Shed
Qay'llnagaay
Heritage Centre

0   0.25   0.5

Scale in kilometres

Loop, which goes around both lakes. Continuing straight on at the junction leads to the Lake Connector Loop, which affords views of both lakes without actually having to walk around them. From the Lake Connector Loop, there is another opportunity to join the Spirit Lake Loop. Look for salal and huckleberries along the trail. Another plant found here is the Indian helebore, used by the Haida for treating various medical problems, including cancer. Note that this trail can be quite muddy at times, especially in the boggy section between the two lakes.

TRAIL 11: SLEEPING BEAUTY

Distance:	**1.5km one way (linear)**
Time:	**4hrs 30mins return**
Rating:	**difficult**
Elevation:	**500m**
Maps:	**NTS 103F/8**
Base:	**Queen Charlotte City**
Best Time:	**May–October**

Note: At the time of printing this trail was temporarily closed by the Ministry of Forests due to budget cuts. Hopefully, the community will soon have this beloved trail officially re-opened. However, the trail still exists (it is only the signs that have been removed), so ask locals for clear directions and conditions of the trail.

Access

From Queen Charlotte City, go north of the Forest Service Office on Cemetery Road and follow the Honna Forest Road for 5km. Turn right across the Honna Road Bridge and follow signs indicating the turn-off and route up Sleeping Beauty. Park your vehicle when the road takes a turn in the bowl. The trailhead is marked with a sign beside the boardwalk in the corner.

Trail Description

This trail is well marked with red markers on trees. It is steep, but pays off with great views. Take water, as there is none on the way. There is a small lake at the top, but drinking the water is not recommended. The trail leads up to Mount Genevieve (also called Sleeping Beauty because the mountain resembles the silhouette of a woman lying down). In early summer, the hillside is a spectacular display of colour, blooming with arnica, shooting stars, single delight and heathers. The trail finally levels out at the bowl, with a beautiful pond in a grassy meadow with purple asters and cotton grass. The final ascent begins with steps cut into a grassy bank. The trail then climbs

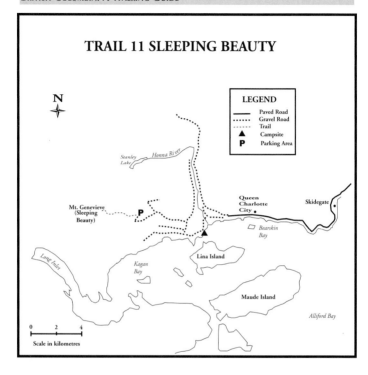

TRAIL 11 SLEEPING BEAUTY

LEGEND

——	Paved Road
······	Gravel Road
- - - -	Trail
▲	Campsite
P	Parking Area

through a forest of stunted, twisted mountain hemlock. It is only a short distance along the ridge to the peak, with great views of the inlet including Queen Charlotte City and Sandspit.

TRAIL 12: RILEY CREEK AND RENNELL SOUND

Distance:	2.5km one way (linear)
Time:	1hr return + extra time on beach (linear)
Rating:	easy–moderate
Maps:	NTS 103F/10, 103F/8

Base:	Queen Charlotte City
Best time:	May–October

Tide tables recommended

The west coast of Haida Gwaii has some of the most rugged shoreline in British Columbia, and its scenic beauty is matchless.

Camping in Rennell Sound
Rennell Sound Forest Service Recreation Site
Access is via logging roads
7 sites, dry toilets, fire pits, boat launch

Cone Head Forest Service Recreation Site
Access is via logging roads
3 sites, dry toilets, fire pits, picnic tables

Access
Access to this trail is via an active logging road, and a 4-wheel drive vehicle is recommended. (Just before Rennell Sound is a very steep hill with a 24% grade that can be difficult to get back up with a 2-wheel drive car, especially after periods of rain.) If you plan to travel Monday to Friday 6.30am to 5.30pm, you must first call the logging company, Weyerhauser, in Juskatla (tel. (250) 557-6810). It is long distance, but call them collect and they will accept the charges. From Queen Charlotte City, take the logging Main Line 22km to Rennell Sound Road. From here, it is about 15km to Rennell Sound, which is at the bottom of the steep hill. Turn right and drive 16km, passing the Forest Service campsites and the log sort until you reach the parking area for the Riley Creek Trail. Drive a little further to reach Gregory Beach and Bonanza Beach, both beautiful and good for beach combing.

Trail Description
Riley Creek
The trailhead sign is high on a tree on the beach side of the road. This short 2.5km trail follows down to the pebble beach. Far beyond

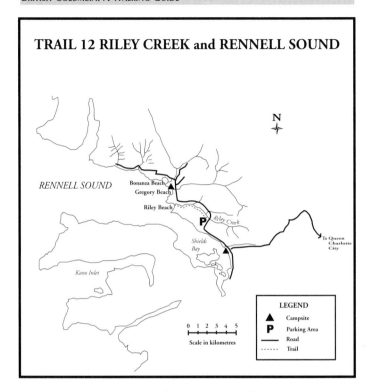

where the eye can see, past the seemingly endless Pacific Ocean, is Japan. The beach is a great place to find shells and other treasures, contemplate life and just linger. The west coast is the only place on Haida Gwaii to see the sun set into the Pacific.

NAIKOON PROVINCIAL PARK

Natural History
Naikoon Provincial Park comprises 72,641 hectares of the northeast tip of Graham Island. The park protects sandy beaches, sphagnum

bogs, sand dunes, old-growth forests, rivers and oceans. Haida people have lived, fished and hunted here for thousands of years and have many legends associated with Tow Hill and Rose Spit, the sand and gravel spit which extends off Rose Point for 12km. The Haidas called Rose Point Nai, and the spit was Naikun, 'The long nose of Nai'. Rose Spit is formed as ocean currents carry sands north from Cape Ball and other exposed cliffs on the east coast. When the waters of Hecate Strait meet the waters of Dixon Entrance, the sand is deposited forming Rose Spit. Parts of the spit are dry and the rest is dangerously shallow – bad for boats but excellent for observing migrating birds on the Pacific Flyway. The upwelling currents produce an abundance of food along the spit, which attracts pelagic species rarely seen from shore. In one of the Haida creation stories, after the great flood had receded and even the strip of sand at Rose Point was dry, Raven flew there and, after eating all the clams and mussels and fishes he found there, he got bored and called out to the empty sky. It is then that he heard the cry from the clamshell that was filled with squirming creatures. And Raven, using his voice to make the most beautiful sounds on earth, coaxed the strange creatures out of their shell. These were the first people, the Haida.

Tow Hill is the 500ft hill facing out to sea. It is a cliff composed of columnar basalt that underwent glaciation from the southeast, and today it reveals important events in geological history, having withstood the forces of ice, storms and ocean tides. The rest of the park is mainly low and flat. The landscape was formed from deposits left by melt waters from glaciers in the last ice age. Most of the park is low bog lands surrounded by red and yellow cedar and lodge pole pine. The Tlell River is famous for its Coho salmon and steelhead trout runs. Small herds of wild cattle have been seen in the park, remnants of early settlement days. In the early 1900s, the BC government encouraged settlers to farm in the Queen Charlottes. Many chose this area to homestead. Most of them were forced to abandon their efforts before the Great Depression because of poor drainage, poor access, lack of markets and World War I. Sitka blacktail deer can be seen everywhere – they were introduced about 80 years ago and, with abundant forage and no wild predators, to say they have prospered would be an understatement. The deer are stripping the forest floor and impacting forest regeneration. The scarcity of young cedars on

Haida Gwaii is of serious concern to the Haida people as cedar is an integral part of their tradition and culture. The sand dunes on East Beach and North Beach are a rarely seen landform in BC. Unlike the dunes of the Sahara Desert, the sandy dunes on Haida Gwaii have an abundance of plant life. The diversity of the plants growing on the dunes helps to stabilize them and fix them in place. The park is committed to protect the dunes in an attempt to preserve the diversity of life found there. It is highly likely that the Haida people have used every area Naikoon Park in the past; every area should be treated with respect as a potential archaeological site.

Camping in Naikoon Provincial Park
Misty Meadows (near Tlell)
30 sites + 10 tent sites, water, firewood, dry toilets, picnic tables, cooking shelter

Agate Beach (near North Beach and Tow Hill)
32 sites + 10 tent sites, water, fire pits, dry toilets, cooking shelter, picnic tables

TRAIL 13: PESUTA TRAIL

Distance:	**10km return (linear)**
Time:	**3hrs 30mins – 4hrs**
Rating:	**easy**
Elevation:	**minimal**
Maps:	**NTS 103G/12**
Base:	**Tlell**
Best time:	**May–October**

Tide tables needed

The *Pesuta* was a 200ft log carrier that was swept ashore during a gale in 1928. The wooden barge was under tow in Hecate Strait when its line parted in the storm. The barge and its logs became driftwood. Each year a little more of the shipwreck disappears. Driftwood on

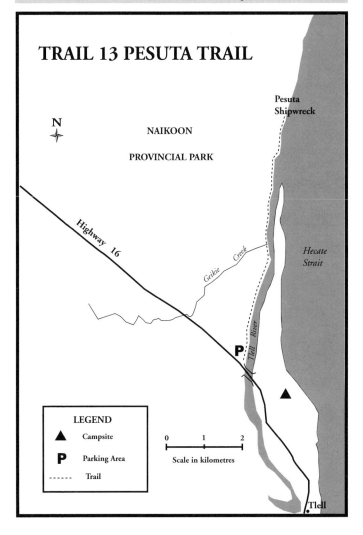

TRAIL 13 PESUTA TRAIL

Pesuta
Shipwreck

N

NAIKOON

PROVINCIAL PARK

Highway 16

Geikie Creek

Hecate
Strait

Tlell River

P

▲

LEGEND

▲ Campsite

P Parking Area

----- Trail

0   1   2

Scale in kilometres

Tlell

The Pesuta *shipwreck, East Beach, near Tlell*

Haida Gwaii is largely a human-made phenomena – almost all drift-wood has been lost from log booms over the past 60 years.

This trail must be taken on an out-going tide, as the river comes up to the dune cliffs and hikers may get stranded while waiting for the river to drop.

Access
In Tlell, just north of the Naikoon Park Headquarters and Visitor Centre, turn into the parking area on the north side of the Tlell River Bridge. The trailhead is the bulletin board, which has information posted about the East Beach hike as well as the current tide tables.

Trail Description
The trail leads north past the outhouses and goes along the ridge parallel to the river. Although most saplings along the trail are hemlock, the forest is mainly spruce with a bit of alder and red cedar.

Sphagnum moss can be seen in the forest. In the spring, rose-purple fairy slippers colour the forest floor; in autumn, large mushrooms, both edible (*boletus*) and poisonous yet beautiful (*Amanita muscaria*), abound. Turn left at the East Beach/Tlell River sign and follow the trail down the short but steep incline to the boardwalk, which crosses swampy lowlands. The trail then reaches the Geikie Creek Bridge. The water is frothy and dark brown due to the tannin released from the bogs upstream. The trail soon meets the trail along the river. If the tide is rising and it is a day with very high tides, on the way back this river trail will be flooded and it will be necessary to wait on the beach until it drops again. Follow the river trail, which can be slippery on the smooth muddy areas – walk closer to the dunes where it is sandy. The sign 'Pesuta Shipwreck 2.5km' marks the halfway point. After this, the trail passes three private properties – do not trespass. The trail from here is along the beach, and agates, petrified wood, shells, sponges and fishing floats are all common finds. The triangular bow of the *Pesuta*, all that remains today, can clearly be seen as you near the mouth of the river. A short walk along the beach and around the driftwood brings you to the shipwreck.

TRAIL 14: EAST BEACH – TLELL RIVER TO ROSE SPIT

Distance:	89km
Time:	4–7 days
Rating:	moderate
Elevation:	minimal change
Maps:	NTS 103G/12-13, 103J/04
Base:	Tlell
Best time:	May–October

Tide tables needed

Access
In Tlell, just north of the Naikoon Park Headquarters and Visitor Centre, turn into the parking area on the north side of the Tlell River Bridge. The trailhead is the bulletin board that has information posted

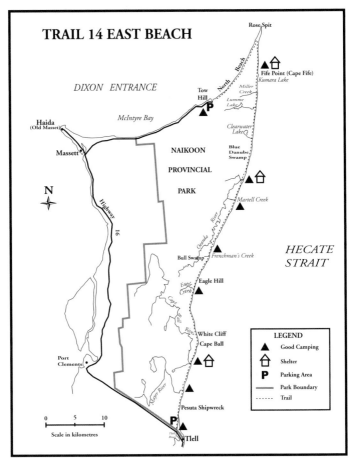

TRAIL 14 EAST BEACH

DIXON ENTRANCE

Rose Spit

Fife Point (Cape Fife)
Kumara Lake

Tow Hill
P

North Beach

Miller Creek

Lumme Lake

McIntyre Bay

Haida (Old Masset)

Clearwater Lake

Massett

Blue Danube Swamp

NAIKOON

PROVINCIAL

PARK

N

Martell Creek

Oeanda River

HECATE STRAIT

Highway 16

Bull Swamp
Frenchman's Creek

Eagle Creek

Eagle Hill

Cape Ball River

White Cliff
Cape Ball

Port Clements

Tlell River

Pesuta Shipwreck

P

Tlell

LEGEND	
▲	Good Camping
⌂	Shelter
P	Parking Area
——	Park Boundary
------	Trail

0   5   10
Scale in kilometres

about the East Beach hike as well as the current tide tables.

Tips
• This trail is best hiked south to north to keep the prevailing wind, rain and sun out of hikers' eyes.

- Hikers should self-register with the RCMP in Masset or Queen Charlotte City and check in on their return. BC Parks does not facilitate a visitor registration programme and will not coordinate any search efforts. There are no shortcuts off East Beach, and sea rescue is difficult. Be prepared.

- Carry water, as it is often scarce. All rivers are tidally influenced for long distances inland, so potable water is usually only available from them at low tide. It is especially difficult to find water between Fife Point and the Hiellen River. Many creeks marked on the topographical maps are either intermittent or enter the ocean underneath the beach.

- There are a number of private properties and environmentally sensitive areas adjacent to the beaches. Respect them.

- A plastic tarp is useful as a kitchen shelter and a rain catcher. Water is usually brown, but safe to drink if boiled or purified.

Trail Description

The trail begins at the picnic site after the Tlell River Bridge and follows the Pesuta Trail for the first 5km. A couple of hours north of the Pesuta is the Cape Ball River, a good place to camp. There is a shelter here as well. Respect the private properties that are inland. The tide floods the mouth of this river, which can only be crossed at low tide. Make sure to leave the Cape Ball River on a receding tide as the sea floods to the base of the 60m sand cliffs along this section. The trek around this headland north to Eagle Hill may take up to 5 hours. Eagle Creek is the only break in this wall that allows a retreat from incoming waves. There are nice camping spots at Eagle Creek. From Eagle Creek to the Oeanda River is about 6hrs 30mins. Again, a low tide is necessary for the steep cliffs and to cross streams. From here to Miller Creek is 5 hours. Tides below 17ft are necessary to pass the steep cliffs. Camp at Miller Creek or else walk a further 30 minutes to the shelter. Near Kumara Lake the sand dunes become prominent. There is another shelter at Fife Point. Those wishing to cut the hike a little short can hike to Tow Hill via the Cape Fife Trail. Cape Fife is where settlers once found gold in the sand. Continue on to Rose Spit. Rose Spit is an ecological reserve and a weather station. From Rose Spit to the Hiellen River and Tow Hill is about 3hrs 30 mins.

The beach at Tlell, on Haida Gwaii

Good camping: Misty Meadows, the Mayer River, Cape Ball River, Eagle Creek, Frenchman Creek, Mortell Creek, Oeanda River, Kumara Lake, east of Tow Hill

Shelters: Cape Ball River, Oeanda River, near Fife Point

Major river crossings: the Mayer, the Cape Ball, the Oeanda – can all be easily waded across their mouths at low tide

Bird watching: Rose Spit, Tlell Beach, meadows near park HQ

Distances: Tlell Bridge to Tow Hill via Rose Spit – 89km
Tlell bridge to outfall of Tlell River – 4km
Outfall of Tlell to Mayer River Outfall – 4.5km
Mayer River to Cape Ball River – 6km
Cape Ball River to Oeanda River – 36.5km
Oeanda River to Cape Fife Trail Head – 17km

Cape Fife Trail Head to Tow Hill via base of Rose
  Spit – 21km
Cape Fife Trail to Tow Hill – 10km

Alternatives

It is possible to cycle on North Beach – it is like riding on pavement;
just make sure to wash the bike afterwards to prevent salt water corro-
sion.

It is possible to drive on East Beach with a 4-wheel drive.

TRAIL 15: TOW HILL/BLOW HOLE

Time:	**1hr 30mins return**
Rating:	**moderate**
Map:	**NTS 103J/4**
Base:	**Massett**
Best time:	**May–October**

Tide tables needed

Tow Hill is a 500ft hill facing out to sea. It was formed by a vertical
lava flow and is made up of columnar basalt. At the base of Tow Hill
is a rocky outcrop. At mid-tide the seawater rushes in as the waves
crash, and the water is forced up through the gaps in the rocks to
form a natural fountain known as the Blow Hole.

There are many Haida legends associated with Tow Hill. In one,
cruel Tow threw down boulders to slay the Haida warrior Hopi. Tow,
underestimating his own powers, fell, leaving his fingerholes in the
rocks below. Tow's pet whale tried to stop Hopi but accidentally ran
himself ashore and turned to stone. The only functioning part of the
whale left is the blow-hole. In another legend, Tow was very greedy
and ate everything in sight including the children of Tlielang. The
blow-hole is what remains of the whale that Tow sent to swallow
Hopi, the villager who finally beat him.

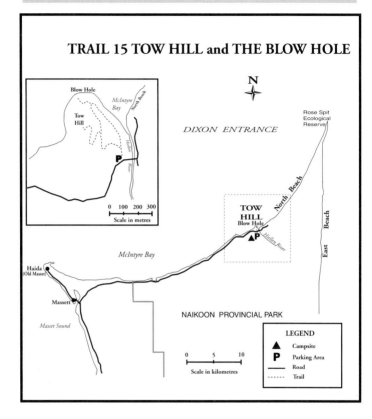

TRAIL 15 TOW HILL and THE BLOW HOLE

N

Blow Hole

McIntyre Bay

North Beach

Tow Hill

Hiellen River

P

DIXON ENTRANCE

Rose Spit Ecological Reserve

0   100 200 300
Scale in metres

TOW HILL
Blow Hole
▲**P**

North Beach

Hiellen River

East Beach

McIntyre Bay

Haida
(Old Masset)

Massett

Masset Sound

NAIKOON PROVINCIAL PARK

0   5   10
Scale in kilometres

LEGEND

▲ Campsite
P Parking Area
—— Road
······ Trail

Access
Tow Hill is a well-posted, partly paved, partly gravelled 26km drive from Masset. Just past Agate Beach Campground, Tow Hill comes into view. Park just before the Hiellen River Bridge. The trailhead is the sign 'Tow Hill Viewpoint' near the bulletin board.

Trail Description
The trail leads past picnic tables and onto a boardwalk. Follow the sign for the Tow Hill Lookout. The trail immediately starts to climb.

Tow Hill, Naikoon Provincial Park

The boardwalk is covered with roofing to prevent slipping and is almost continuous to the summit. The trail is a series of switchbacks, and it passes a huge burl as it climbs through the mainly spruce forest. A platform affords a great view of North Beach and, if it is a clear day, the Coast Mountains on the mainland. The platform at the top of Tow Hill faces west overlooking Agate Beach and Yakoun Point and, inland, Mendham's Muskeg. Walk down the same way until you reach the sign 'Tow Hill/Blow Hole'. A short hike down a slightly steeper and muddier boardwalk leads to the sign 'Tow Hill View Point' pointing back the way you came. The trail drops to the beach almost directly in front of the blow-hole. A 20-minute walk on the boardwalk along the Hiellen River leads back to the parking area.

TRAIL 16: CAPE FIFE TRAIL

Time:	7hrs or overnight
Rating:	moderate
Map:	NTS 103J/4
Base:	Massett
Best Time:	April–October

Tide tables needed

Access
The trailhead can be reached from Masset by a 26km partly paved, partly gravelled road. Just past Agate Beach Campground and the parking for Tow Hill and across the Hiellen River Bridge, a sign on the right indicates the trailhead.

Trail Description
The Cape Fife Trail is an overnight backpacking trip for experienced hikers. Take water, as there is none on the way. The trail, which cuts across to East Beach, follows an early settlers' road for part of the way. In the early days of European settlement, settlers began homesteading in the bogs near Tow Hill. The trail follows the old settlers' path through the forest that changes from spruce to hemlock to cedar.

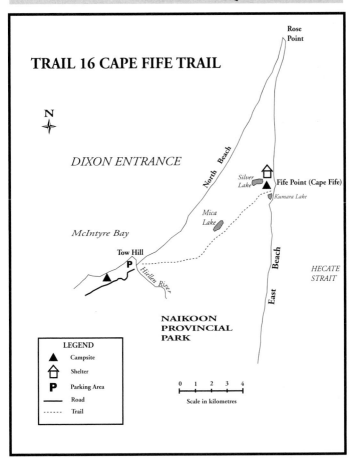

TRAIL 16 CAPE FIFE TRAIL

Rose Point

N

DIXON ENTRANCE

North Beach

Silver Lake

Fife Point (Cape Fife)

Kumara Lake

Mica Lake

McIntyre Bay

Tow Hill

P

Hiellen River

East Beach

HECATE STRAIT

NAIKOON PROVINCIAL PARK

LEGEND

▲ Campsite

⌂ Shelter

P Parking Area

— Road

····· Trail

0 1 2 3 4

Scale in kilometres

Look out for vestiges of the corduroy road built just after World War I. The original trail was just a little way to north of the present-day trail and was the 1912 wagon road to the settlement at Kumara Lake. In 1972, the Massett Haida Lions Club cleared the trail, and in 1985 Parks Canada built boardwalks in many areas. There is a small, rustic,

three-sided shelter at Cape Fife, and good protected tent sites at Cape
Fife and Rumera Creek. It can be very cold and windy at Cape Fife –
be prepared. The Cape Fife Trail is the only access to this part of the
east coast except via the beaches. Gray whales can often be seen in
April.

Alternative
An alternative is to go north from the trail exit up to Rose Spit. Rose
Spit is an ecological reserve – unusual birds and sea lions can be
seen here. From Rose Spit, walk west to Tow Hill.

Note on Bogs in Naikoon
The bogs in Naikoon Provincial Park illustrate a continuous cycle of
change and provide excellent examples of sphagnum bog communities. Some are raised bogs, in which layer upon layer of mosses grow
and decay, forming raised beds or hummocks. These hummocks
provide a drier environment where pines and shrubs can survive. A
bog forest may then develop. The appearance of the bog will change;
the forest may die and revert back to small ponds where mosses will
again flourish.

GWAII HAANAS NATIONAL PARK RESERVE/
HAIDA HERITAGE SITE

Gwaii Haanas, 'Islands of beauty', with its unique and spectacular
scenery, is located in the south of Haida Gwaii. It contains 138 islands
and 1600km of shoreline, and covers an area of 1470 hectares. In
1988, the area was designated as a national park reserve in recognition of its rich natural and cultural heritage. Accessible only by water
or air, Gwaii Haanas has been home to the Haida for thousands of
years and continues to be of great spiritual, cultural and economic
significance. There are more than 500 Haida archaeological and
historical sites here, including villages and burial caves. The village
of Nan Sdins (previously known as Ninstints) on SGaang Gwaay has
the world's finest display of Haida mortuary poles, all of which are
over 100 years old. In 1981, UNESCO declared Nan Sdins, 'The one
who is two,' a world heritage site.

Gwaii Haanas is jointly managed by the Council of the Haida Nation and Parks Canada. Together they are known as the Archipelago Management Board, and they share all aspects of planning, management and operations. In Haida legends, the role of the watchmen was to alert their owner to the approach of an enemy or any other happening he should be aware of. Watchmen are symbolized by three human figures wearing high hats, often found on the top of Haida totem poles. To protect culturally significant sites, a Watchmen programme was initiated in the 1970s. In the past, people, museums and the government have stolen totem poles from Gwaii Haanas, and beams from houses have been used for firewood. Because of this, several Haida people moved back to the old villages in the 1970s as the first Haida Gwaii Watchmen, and Haida Watchmen can be found at five of the old village sites. It is recognized that the protection of Gwaii Haanas is essential to sustaining Haida culture. Today, this protection is achieved mainly by educating visitors about the natural and cultural heritage of Gwaii Haanas and by ensuring that the visitors leave no trace.

Visitors to Gwaii Haanas must make a reservation and attend a mandatory orientation session prior to departure. Call Super Natural British Columbia (tel. 1-800-663-6000 or, if outside North America, (250) 387-1642). A quota system is in place to manage visitor impacts on the natural and cultural features and to preserve the experience of wilderness solitude. The limit is 12 people on shore at any one time within sight or sound of each other. The orientation covers public safety, no-trace camping practices, marine and other hazards, natural and cultural heritage, and the Haida Gwaii Watchmen programme.

Gwaii Haanas is remote wilderness and is accessible only by boat or chartered aircraft. It cannot be overstressed that independent travel is safe only for self-reliant experienced marine travellers. For more information, contact the Gwaii Haanas office at Box 37, Queen Charlotte City, BC, V0T 1S0, tel. (250) 559-8818. There are many tour companies that go into Gwaii Haanas by either water or air. A few suggestions are:

Aay Oo Guiding Services
Tel. (250) 559-0061 or 1-877-262-9929
Fax (250) 559-0071
www.aayoo.com

Anvil Cove Charters
Keith and Barb Rowsell
Box 454, Queen Charlotte City, BC
V0T 1S0
Tel./Fax (250) 559-8207
Email: anvilcov@qcislands.net

Moresby Explorers
Box 109, Sandspit, BC, V0T 1T0
Tel. (250) 637-2215 or 1-800-806-7633
Email: doug@moresbyexplorers.com

Queen Charlotte Adventures
Box 196, Queen Charlotte City, BC, V0T 1S0
Tel. (250) 559-8990 or 1-800-668-4288

Takuli III Sailing Adventures
Tel. (250) 559-8667
www.qcislands.net/takuli
Email: takuli@qcislands.net

South Moresby Air Charters
Tel. (250) 559-4222 or 1-888-551-4222
www.smair.com

Resources
A free Gwaii Haanas Information Package is available from Super Natural BC (tel. 1-800-663-6000) or www.harbour.com/parkscan/gwaii or by calling the Gwaii Haanas office at (250) 559-8818.

Queen Charlotte Observer newspaper website: www.qciobserver.com

Guide to the Queen Charlotte Islands – a comprehensive publication updated annually containing maps, accommodation and service information. It is available free from the Queen Charlotte Visitor Information Centre, Box 819, Queen Charlotte, BC, V0T 1S0, Tel. (250) 559-8316, Fax (250) 559-8952, Email: info@qcinfo.com.

Natural Bridge in Yoho National Park

Serenity in northern British Columbia (photo by Martijn Coini)

Trail through the forest (photo by Martijn Coini)

WHISTLER AND SQUAMISH

History

The traditional territory of the Squamish Nation included most of the Lower Mainland of British Columbia, including Vancouver, Burnaby, New Westminister, North and West Vancouver, Port Moody, Squamish and Whistler. Some of the village sites date back 8000 years, and the Squamish Nations have been occupying their land continuously since this time, uninterrupted by the arrival of the Europeans. Despite the intense pressure of massive urban development, they have never ceded or surrendered their aboriginal title. The Squamish Nation is made up of seven communities and 2700 people living mainly in reserves in Mission, Capilano, Seymour and throughout the Squamish valley. Squamish means 'Mother of the wind' in Coast Salish language.

The Sea-to-Sky Highway (Highway 99), which links Vancouver to Squamish and Whistler, traces a major overland trade route that linked the coastal Squamish peoples and interior Lil'wat peoples. Horseshoe Bay, where the BC Ferries terminal is, was a camping place for people travelling between present-day Squamish and the Burrard Inlet. Some 8km north of Squamish, the highway follows the Cheakamus River, 'Salmon weir place'. This salmon-rich conflence of two rivers was once the site of several Squamish villages. Near Brackendale, the highway offers several viewpoints to watch the thousands of eagles that rest here in winter. A few kilometres north of Brackendale, the name Cheekeye, meaning 'Dirty place', was given to the muddy river and the mountain now known as Garibaldi. During the great flood, the Squamish people lashed their canoes to this 2678m high peak.

Today, Whistler is a premier skiing and snowboarding resort, with a bustling nightlife to go with it. The village itself offers shops and restaurants of all kinds, outdoor bars and cafes with a stunning view of Whistler and Blackcomb mountains. There is a nice one-hour walk from the village around Lost Lake. The lake has a picnic area and a wooden dock that jets out into the water, a great place to swim in warmer weather. Long after many of the ski resorts have closed for the season, the highest parts of Whistler are still open for skiing and

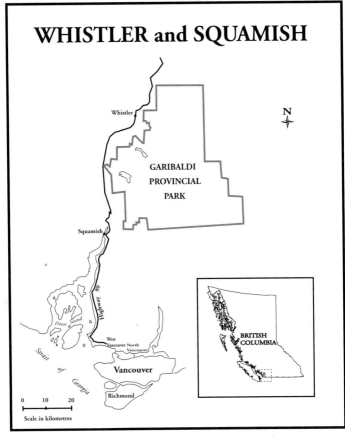

WHISTLER and SQUAMISH

Whistler

N

GARIBALDI

PROVINCIAL

PARK

Squamish

Highway 99

Howe Sound

West
Vancouver North
Vancouver

Strait

Vancouver

BRITISH
COLUMBIA

of

Georgia

Richmond

0   10   20

Scale in kilometres

snowboarding, so don't be surprised on a hot spring day to see some
people sunbathing in shorts, and others walking around in their full
snowboarding gear!

There is a plethora of high-priced resorts and hotels, but that need
not put off budget travellers. Although only a short drive from
Vancouver, it is well worth spending a few days here. There are
cheaper options, lots of campgrounds and a grocery store in the

village to buy food. The library offers free internet – just sign up for a time slot.

Getting There
Squamish and Whistler are both on the Sea-to-Sky Highway (Highway 99), north of Vancouver. From downtown Vancouver, drive through Stanley Park heading for the Lions Gate Bridge over to North and West Vancouver. Follow the signs towards Horseshoe Bay and then for Highway 99. Whistler is about 120km from Vancouver, with Squamish about halfway up. Maverick Coach Lines from the Greyhound Bus depot in Vancouver and BC Rail both service Squamish and Whistler.

Whistler Accommodation
Hostelling International – Whistler
5678 Alta Lake Road
Whistler, BC
V0N 1B0
Tel: (604) 932-5492
Email: whistler@hihostels.bc.ca

Directions: Heading from Vancouver on Highway 99, turn left on Alta Road once you have entered Whistler, but before you reach the village. The hostel is 4.8km from the highway turn-off on the right side of the road.

This is a great hostel in a big rustic timber lodge right on Alta Lake with a beautiful view of the mountains. It's only a five-minute drive to the village and there's plenty to do right here. Take out a canoe for free, get some local tips off the very helpful and friendly staff or just sit on the back porch and enjoy the scenery.

Shoestring Lodge
7124 Nancy Green Drive
Tel: (604) 932-3338

If the hostel is fully booked, as it often is, then this is a good second option (besides camping). It's on Highway 99 on the right-hand side just a bit past the main village entrances.

View of the Whistler area

TRAIL 17: STAWAMUS CHIEF

Distance:	6km
Time:	1–2hrs one way
Elevation change:	600m
Rating:	moderate–difficult
Map:	NTS 92G/11
Base:	Vancouver or Whistler

Access

Stawamus Chief Provincial Park is located adjacent to Shannon Falls Provincial Park with gravel road access. From Vancouver, drive north on Highway 99 to Squamish – the park access is 1km before Squamish. Turn right onto the old road above the viewpoint and park at the end.

Background

Stawamus Chief is a steep face of rock at the head of Howe Sound –
at 652m it is the second highest piece of granite in the world and
attracts expert international climbers. There is a story about a giant
serpent that is very significant both culturally and historically to the
Squamish peoples. The serpent slithered across Howe Sound and then
left its track across this steep rock face. Stawamus Chief is named
after the Squamish village of Sta-a-mus, located at the north end of
the Squamish River. Although this is an extremely popular place to
hike and climb, the trail is very steep and requires physical fitness
and sturdy footwear. Make sure to bring some water, as there is very
little shade along the steep trail.

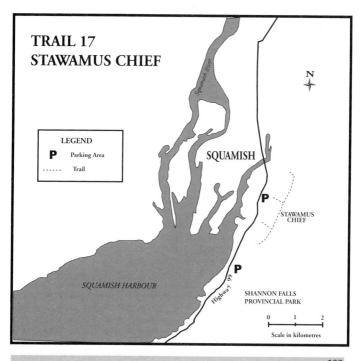

TRAIL 17
STAWAMUS CHIEF

N

LEGEND

P   Parking Area

------   Trail

Squamus River

SQUAMISH

P

STAWAMUS
CHIEF

P

SQUAMISH HARBOUR

Highway 99

SHANNON FALLS
PROVINCIAL PARK

0   1   2

Scale in kilometres

Trailhead to the Top

Climb over the large boulder located at the base of the trail and start climbing the steps. The staircase is very steep but there are handrails. The staircase was built in 1985 by the Federation of BC Mountain Clubs. At Olesen Creek, there's a bridge over to the Shannon Falls Trail. There is a bench here and a good view over Howe Sound. From here there are three peaks, and hikers can choose one that is suited to their fitness level. Take the wood and stone stairs that lead up beside Olesen Creek. Part of the staircase is made up of roots – in the past, hikers had to pull themselves up through the roots of the trees! After about 20 minutes, the trail leaves the creek behind and then the divides. The upper left fork goes to the three peaks and the right fork leads to Stawamus Squaw, a companion peak to the Chief, 2 hours away. Some 20 minutes later, the trail divides again just past a huge boulder perching on a ledge. This ledge is the first viewpoint, and the rock face looks like a granite wall streaked with colours from oxidizing minerals. This is in contrast to the interior of the rock, which can be seen in split boulders at the bottom of the Chief – it is bright white with black dots.

The trail is mostly smooth and wide. Near the top above the tree line is an open, windswept spot. From the top, there is an excellent view of Shannon Falls to the south and to the north; the Squamish River cuts through the valley between Howe Sound and Brackendale. To the west, across the water, is the Tantalus Range on Vancouver Island with its stunning glaciated peaks. Make sure to wear appropriate footwear, as the descent is steep.

Hikers wishing to explore this area further may stay at one of the 15 drive-in campsites or 45 wilderness/walk-in campsites. There is also a day-use picnic area.

Alternatives

The Shannon Falls Provincial Park is adjacent. A short, easy trail through the forest leads to Shannon Falls, a spectacular 340m falls plummeting down a granite bluff. The Squamish people believe it was formed when a huge sea monster crashed into the coast in the futile pursuit of a giant eagle. The falls are BC's third highest waterfall.

TRAIL 18: BLACK TUSK/GARIBALDI LAKE

Distance:	**9km one way (to Garibaldi Lake)**
Time:	**3–4hrs one way (to Garibaldi Lake)**
Rating:	**moderate**
Elevation change:	**810m (to Garibaldi Lake)**
Maps:	**NTS 92G14/92G15**
Best time:	**August–September**

No other rock formation in the Coast Mountains is as noticeable as the Black Tusk. It is a pillar of volcanic rock standing 2316m high, a remnant of a large lava flow that vented on these slopes. To the Squamish people, the Black Tusk, Tak-tak-a-moh-yin-tla-ain-ain-ya-ha-an, was known as 'The landing place of the Thunderbird'. They believed that the magical Thunderbird lived on the top, flapping its wings to cause thunder and shooting lightning bolts from its eyes. They observed a strict taboo against climbing any of the mountains.

The Garibaldi Lake Trail leads to a beautiful turquoise lake formed by volcanoes and glaciers. In late summer, alpine meadows bloom in every colour possible, with the lower elevations covered with a dense forest of western red cedar, western hemlock and Douglas fir. Seldom seen but present nonetheless are deer, mountain goats, black bears, grizzly bears and golden eagles. This park may have snow until late July or August – the ski and snowboard season lasts until mid-June!

Access

Garibaldi Provincial Park has several access points. For Garibaldi Lake, turn right off Highway 99 just after you cross the Rubble Creek Bridge. This is 37km north of Squamish and 19km south of Whistler. Watch for the 'Black Tusk' sign. A 2.5km paved road leads east to the Rubble Creek parking area and trailhead. Due to the instability of the Barrier, the 1000ft high lava wall rising above Rubble Creek, there is a ban on overnight parking in the parking area. The Barrier is a broad wall of red volcanic rock formed when a flow of molten lava, meeting a glacier that once occupied Rubble Creek, cooled and hardened to create a thick rock face that holds back the waters of Garibaldi Lake.

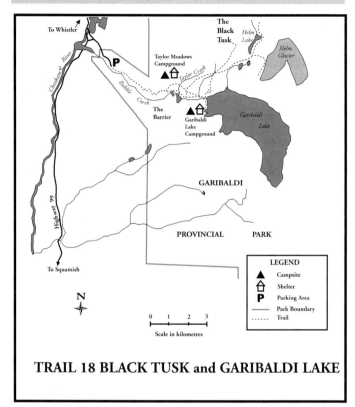

TRAIL 18 BLACK TUSK and GARIBALDI LAKE

Trail Description

The trail starts at the southeast corner of the parking area beside Rubble Creek. The banks of Rubble Creek are lined with boulders left from the last great slide. The waters are frothy white in late summer when snowmelt is at its peak. The first 4km of the trail are fairly easy, and the first 2.5km run parallel with the creek – the trail starts straight and changes to switchbacks further up the mountain. This part takes about an hour. Notice that the Douglas firs and red cedars that line the beginning of the trail are smaller than the ones farther up. This is because of the great landslide in 1855 that wiped out most of the lower forest. There aren't any views from the trail until around 6km. There is a small shelter here and a map. The trail to the left leads up to Taylor Meadows and Black Tusk Meadows. From here, the trail continues straight ahead to Barrier Lake. About 100m ahead, a short trail to the right leads almost immediately to a viewpoint. From the viewpoint, the Barrier is visible. Its visage later in the afternoon is best, as its face is shaded in the morning light. To the southwest is the Tantalus Range rising above the Squamish Valley and around to Powder Mountain above the Callaghan Valley. Just around the corner from the viewpoint is an even more beautiful view of Barrier Lake. In August and September the water levels are at their highest, and sunlight reflecting off the fine sediment in the water results in the most intense blue colour. Behind is Cloudburst Mountain. The trail leads around Barrier Lake to Lesser Garibaldi Lake. Just past the lake, the trail re-enters the forest and divides again just before 8km. The trail to the left goes to the Taylor Meadows Campground. From here it is about 15 minutes to Garibaldi Lake. There is a bridge over Parnasus Creek, and the trail then leads on to the Garibaldi Lake Campground. There are 100 campsites scattered on the hillside above the lake – some of them have wooden platforms on which to pitch a tent. There is a cabin there for the park rangers, who put on interpretive programmes for visitors. There are pit toilets but no refuse containers, so all rubbish must be packed out. There is a $5 per person per night backcountry fee payable at self-registration boxes.

Just offshore of Garibaldi Lake are the Battleship Islands, which are a string of small rocky outcroppings formed by lava flow. When the water levels are low, it is possible to wade out to them or swim. A sign on the lakeside-trail says '9km elevation 1470m'. When the lake levels are at their highest, parts of the boardwalk leading out into the lake double as rafts from which to swim or relax. The trail around the lake goes only a short distance past the campground.

Alternatives
Garibaldi Lake Campground to Black Tusk: 6km, 2–3hrs one way, elevation change 790m, difficult
The only camping is at Garibaldi Lake or Taylor Meadows, so this trail is best done as a side-trip from the campsite. This trail ends on the

shoulder of the Black Tusk. The trail from Garibaldi Lake climbs through the forest above the lake and meets up with the trail from Taylor Meadows after about 30 minutes. The trail passes a series of small ponds dotted on the mountainside. The views from the open meadows change every few minutes as elevation is gained and Garibaldi Lake is visible in its full extent. There's a trailhead marker in Black Tusk Meadows and a pit toilet. From here it is a 3km climb to the Black Tusk, or trails can be taken to Panorama Ridge or Helm Lake. Panorama Ridge is 3km away, with unlimited views of Garibaldi Lake, Sphinx and Sentinel Glaciers, and Table Mountain; the Helm Lake Trail is 14km through a distinctly volcanic zone to Cheakamus Lake.

The 3km trail to the Black Tusk climbs steadily to a nearby ridge. It is very strenuous, but there are beautiful meadows on all sides that bloom with blue lupine, red heather, yellow cinquefoil and Indian paintbrush. In about an hour, the trail reaches the ridge, with views of Black Tusk's south face. Subalpine firs fade away to a barren expanse with a dusty trail leading across the flats. Only properly equipped and experienced climbers should attempt to climb the Tusk. The ascent of the last 100m, by a rock chimney on its south side, must be negotiated very carefully. Many visitors wear helmets – beware of falling rocks.

Taylor Meadows and Garibaldi Lake circuit: 22km, 11hrs, elevation change 915m, moderate–difficult

Another alternative is to take the trail from the Rubble Creek parking area to Taylor Meadows, then back down to Garibaldi Lake and back to the parking area. This makes a long day-hike for ambitious hikers.

Trails 19–21 are short, but can be combined to make a great day of walks to beautiful waterfalls, through various ages of forest stands, and to a lake with a view.

TRAIL 19: BRANDYWINE FALLS

Distance:	**1km return**
Time:	**30mins return**
Base:	**Whistler**
Rating:	**easy**

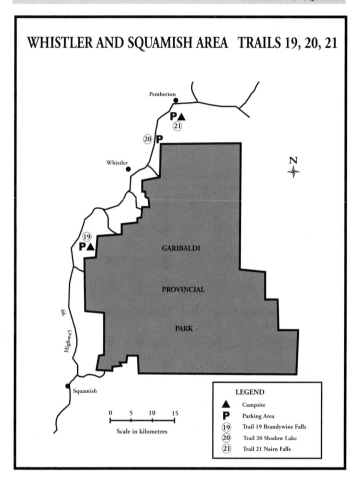

Access

Brandywine Falls Provincial Park is off Highway 99 just south of Whistler and 47km north of Squamish. BC Parks runs a campground here with 15 drive-in sites.

Trail

This is a really short trail, but it is included because the falls are amazing to see. From the parking area, it's about 0.5km to get there. For thousands of years, water cut through layers of lava to create the Brandywine Falls and the swirling plunge pool below them. The falls may only be 70m high but they drain 4300 hectares, an area 30 times the size of the park!

TRAIL 20: SHADOW LAKE

Distance:	**3km return**
Time:	**1hr–1hr 30mins**
Base:	**Whistler**
Rating:	**easy**

Access

Shadow Lake is one of three interpretive forests being developed in the Squamish Forest District. It is located midway between Whistler and Pemberton on Highway 99, about 15km from each. The parking area is on the right-hand side of the highway.

Trail

Cross over the highway from the parking area and follow the directional signs. There are several short trails here: to the right is the High Forestry Trail and Low Forestry Trail. The Shadow Lake Loop Trail is to the left. Follow the trail to the left, passing through natural forest that originated after a forest fire in the mid-1920s. The trail is fairly flat and well marked. The trail goes around the lake and comes to a small bridge. From here there is a good view of the mountains all around. Cross the bridge and continue through the forest and follow the trail to the end. The trail ends at a secluded river with a white sand beach. It's a good place to relax and enjoy the views. Follow the trail back the same way.

TRAIL 21: NAIRN FALLS

Distance:	3km return
Time:	40mins–1hr return
Base:	Whistler
Rating:	easy

Access

Follow Highway 99 about 32km north of Whistler and 3km south of Pemberton. There is a viewpoint off the about 1km before the park

Nairn Falls, near Whistler

entrance. Turn right off the highway into the parking area. There are 94 campsites in the park, and it is an ideal camping base from which to explore the Whistler area.

Background

Nairn Falls has always attracted visitors. The Lillooet peoples first bridged this gap, and then early European settlers crossed here to climb Mount Currie. The Pacific Great Eastern Railway used to bring up trainloads of tourists, and today visitors are drawn to watch the fast-flowing Green River tunnelling its way through granite. Nairn Falls are only 60m high, but it is fascinating to watch and hear the tremendous power of the moving water.

Trail

The 1.5km trail begins at the parking area and heads along a high ridge above the green waters of the river. The path is narrow and can be dangerous when icy. The embankment drops away sharply as the trail cuts through old-growth Douglas fir. An eroded section of the trail runs beside the river. During the floods of August 1991, the Green River washed out some of the riverbank. An alternative trail climbs the hillside above the river. The viewpoints at the end, at Nairn Falls, are fenced off for added security. Watch the Green River plummet over the falls and swirl around boulders, rushing past, dropping again and disappearing into the forest.

Alternatives

2km further north on Highway 99, before Pemberton, is One Mile Lake. This is a good spot for swimming and picnicking.

MANNING PROVINCIAL PARK

Natural History
Manning Provincial Park was established in 1941 to preserve the forests of the Cascade Mountains. It was named in honour of Earnest C. Manning, Chief Forester of British Columbia from 1936 to 1941, when he was killed in an airplane accident. He was dedicated to the preservation and conservation of the Canadian wilderness and was instrumental in developing the idea of setting aside land for future generations to enjoy. Manning Provincial Park is comprised of 65,900 hectares, bordered to the south by the Canada–US boundary where it adjoins North Cascade National Park in Washington. The park protects and contains five of BC's fourteen biogeoclimatic zones, including lush coastal growth, dryland stands of pine, alpine larch and subalpine meadows. Being so close to Vancouver, Manning Provincial Park is a favourite with the city's residents. In winter, it offers supreme cross-country skiing, and in summer endless hiking opportunities, horse trails and camping.

Background
The Interior Salish and Shuswap were the first people in the Okanagan area and have left pithouses and other archaeological finds. Miners came much later, leaving behind historic trails and old railway lines. There is also evidence of trappers and fur traders.

Getting There
From Vancouver, take the TransCanada (Highway 1) east to Hope and then follow the Crowsnest Highway (Highway 3) towards Princeton. Highway 3 passes through the park. The park's west gate is 26km east of Hope, and the park headquarters is exactly halfway between Hope and Princeton, 68km from each. Manning Park is serviced from Vancouver by Greyhound Bus Lines, tel. (604) 840-8857.

Campgrounds
There are 355 campsites in four different campgrounds.

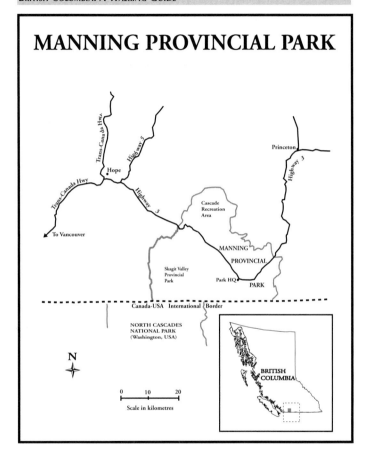

MANNING PROVINCIAL PARK

TRAIL 22: HEATHER TRAIL (TO FIRST BROTHER)

Distance:	20km return
Time:	9hrs return
Rating:	moderate

Elevation change:	292m
Base:	**Hope or Vancouver**
Map:	**NTS 92H/2**
Best time:	**mid-July to mid-August**

These meadows were threatened with overgrazing by domestic sheep, and the urging of the people of the area prompted the creation of the Three Brothers Mountain Reserve in 1931. And then in 1941, these meadows were included in the area declared the Earnest C. Manning Provincial Park. In 1994, reclamation of the meadows was started, and hikers can do their part by obeying all signs and staying off the newly vegetated areas. Meadows are extremely fragile, and even one step off the trail can damage what may have taken up to 20 years to bloom!

Access
From Highway 3, turn off across from the Manning Park Lodge and follow the Blackwall Peak Road to its end, where there are two parking areas. The trail can be started from either of the parking areas as the two trails join after less than 1km.

Trail Description
The trail begins at the base of Blackwall Peak and slowly descends the western slope of Lone Man Ridge. The Three Brothers Mountain comes into view shortly after the start of the hike. As the trail descends into the valley, the surrounding vegetation becomes more and more lush. After 5km, the trail reaches Buckhorn Wilderness Campsite and the descent ends. There is a small stream to get water from. From here, the route crosses a small creek and then begins to climb out of the valley and onto open ridges. The climb from Buckhorn Campsite to Bonnevier Ridge is quite strenuous. The trail winds through an old burn area, a skeleton of a forest where there was a fire in 1945. Blue birds and hawk owls can often be seen around here. The trail then re-emerges above the treeline into the open alpine meadows. During the summer, these meadows are carpeted with brilliant wildflowers, a splendid mix of radiant colour.

Follow the trail towards First Brother; this area of the trail is often covered with snow patches or water. The trail descends and then

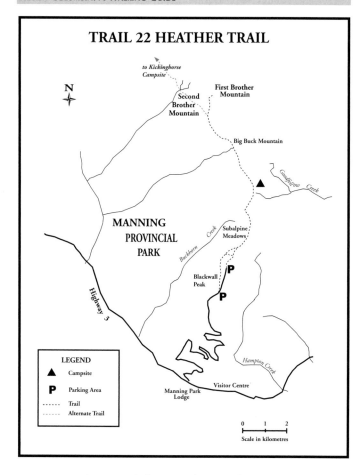

TRAIL 22 HEATHER TRAIL

N

to Kickinghorse Campsite

First Brother Mountain

Second Brother Mountain

Big Buck Mountain

Goodfellow Creek

MANNING PROVINCIAL PARK

Buckhorn Creek

Subalpine Meadows

P

Blackwall Peak

P

Highway 3

Hampton Creek

LEGEND

▲ Campsite

P Parking Area

------ Trail

------ Alternate Trail

Manning Park Lodge

Visitor Centre

0   1   2

Scale in kilometres

enters a very dry area of alpine tundra. At 10km, an orange fluores-cent square marks the route that climbs up to the summit of the First Brother, 2272m. Watch out for moss campion, a bright pink cushion plant that is found only here and on Mount Frosty. With such a short growing season, it spends up to 10 years growing a long tap root to secure itself and capture water before it finally blooms. It is a 1km strenuous climb/scramble over rugged rocky sections to the top of First Brother. Good footwear is required. From the top, Second and Third Brothers can be seen to the west and Blackwall Peak to the south.

Alternatives

For hikers wishing to spend a few days in the meadows, continue west from First Brother. Kickinghorse Wilderness Campsite is 3.5km further on a moderate trail with a few switchbacks. This is a good place to stop for the night. From Kickinghorse, it's 7.5km on high ground to the ridge overlooking Nicomen Lake and then a 2km descent via switchbacks to the Nicomen Lake Wilderness Campsite. Fires are discouraged.

TRAIL 23: SKYLINE 1 TRAIL

Distance:	**20.4km loop**
Time:	**7–9hrs**
Rating:	**difficult**
Elevation change:	775m
Base:	**Vancouver or Hope**
Map:	**NTS 92H/2**
Best Time:	**mid-June to mid-September**

Access

From the Manning Park Lodge on Highway 3, follow the signs to the Strawberry Flats parking area. This trail is often done as a loop with cars left at both ends (Strawberry Flats and Spruce Bay parking areas), but the distance between the two is an easy 3.8km walk along the road or else on the north section of the Gibson Loop Trail.

Trail Description

From the Strawberry Flats parking area, the trail traces the old fire-access road through a forest of mainly lodgepole pine and then through a meadow that blooms with colourful wildflowers all

TRAIL 23 SKYLINE I TRAIL

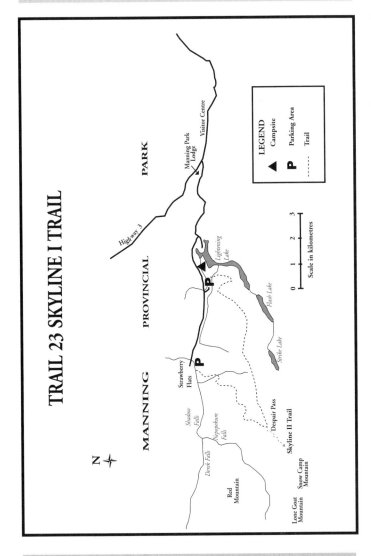

LEGEND

▲ Campsite

P Parking Area

...... Trail

Scale in kilometres

0 1 2 3

N

MANNING   PROVINCIAL   PARK

Highway 3

Manning Park Lodge

Visitor Centre

Lightening Lake

Flash Lake

Strike Lake

Strawberry Flats

Despair Pass

Skyline II Trail

Shadow Falls

Nepopekum Falls

Derek Falls

Snow Camp Mountain

Red Mountain

Lone Goat Mountain

summer. To the west is Red Mountain, 2922m, named for the colour of its exposed iron ore deposits. At about 0.5km, the trail narrows and veers south through dense Engelmann spruce and alpine fir forest. At 3.7km, there is a meadow that begins a popular birdwatching zone; this continues on to the burn area, the result of a forest fire in the 1940s. From the burn area, there's a good view of the valley below. The trail heads onto the drier NNW-facing slope affording views of Red Mountain, Lone Goat Mountain and Snow Camp Mountain. Mount Hozameen, in the USA, can be seen in the distance. Just before 6km, above Despair Pass at the junction with Skyline II Trail, the route takes a sharp turn and gives a brief view of Thunder Lake. From this point, overnight hikers continue 6.5km to the Mowich Wilderness Campsite on the Skyline II Trail (there is no camping permitted on Skyline I Trail), but day-hikers head east on the ridge above the Lightning Lake Chain's valley.

The Skyline I trail passes through a subalpine meadow, which offers a panoramic view of the area and is bursting with vibrant wild-flowers in the summer months. From mid- to late June, the south-facing meadows are carpeted with glacier lily and western anemone; in July, it's lupin, arnica, mountain daisy and paintbrush; and by late August, the colourful bloom is over for another year and all that remains are the flower heads and leaves of the dying plants. After the meadow, the trail stays about 180m below the ridge crest on the south side but rises to the top of the knolls, affording great views. To the north is the Gibson Pass ski area; to the northeast are Blackwall Peak, Cascade Lookout and Three Brothers. For the next 1.25km, the trail enters an area that was cleared for firefighting purposes during the 1994 forest fire. Three areas in this part of the trail were used as heli-pads and water reservoirs. Stay on the trail to protect the new vegeta-tion. After an initial swift descent, the trail slowly winds down to the valley floor. This area is very steep in areas and often wet. Eventually, the trail merges into an old fire-access road, which descends to the Lightning Lake junction. Follow the Lightning Lake Trail 1km east to the Spruce Bay parking area.

Alternatives
Some may prefer to hike this trail the opposite way – the initial eleva-tion gain is more strenuous but the views are amazing.

TRAIL 24: PACIFIC CREST TRAIL/CASTLE CREEK/ MONUMENT 78 LOOP

Distance:	24km return
Time:	8hrs
Rating:	Moderate-Difficult
Elevation change:	450 m
Base:	Vancouver or Hope
Map:	NTS 92H/2
Best Time:	July–September

The Pacific Crest Trail (PCT) is the beginning (or end) of a six-month hiking route to Mexico of just over 4000km. For hikers planning to do the whole PCT, the earliest north–south departure is mid- to late June because of heavy snowfall and dangerous avalanche conditions on the trail just south of the border. All hikers are strongly advised either to do the hike from south to north or else to begin the north–south hike in July. Information and registration for the trail can be obtained from the Manning Park Visitor Centre.

Access
The trail begins from the Beaver Pond/Windy Joe/PCT trailhead parking area, which is located on Highway 3, 500m east of the Manning Park Visitor Centre.

Trail Description
For the first 4.8km, follow the Windy Joe Trail. From the parking area, the trail heads west 500 m before following a dirt road, an old fire-access route. The trail passes through forest, leads over a wooden bridge and then crosses over the Similkameen River via a second steel bridge. At 4.8km, the trail comes to the junction of Windy Joe and the PCT and Frosty Mountain trail. The trail veers right at the junction and reaches a second junction only 1km later. At the second junction, keep left (the right trail leads to Frosty Mountain). The Pacific Crest Wilderness Campsite is 0.5km further. There is a pit toilet and a stream to collect water – there is no water available for the next 5km.

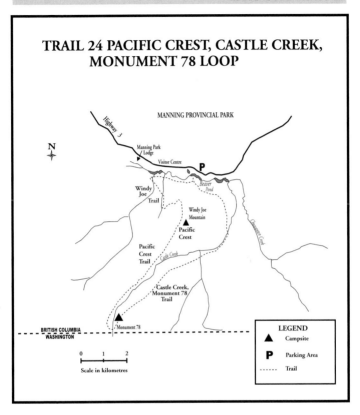

After the campsite, the trail descends to the southwest through colourful meadows offering great views of the surrounding area. The trail crosses Castle Creek to a campsite. The border monument is 500m ahead. The route back via the Castle Creek/Monument 78 Trail follows along Castle Creek passing through several meadows. The trail ends back at Beaver Pond and the same parking area as the Pacific Crest Trail.

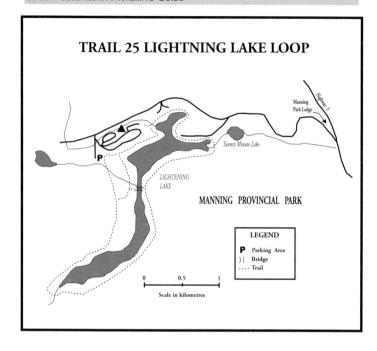

TRAIL 25 LIGHTNING LAKE LOOP

MANNING PROVINCIAL PARK

LEGEND
P Parking Area
)(Bridge
---- Trail

0   0.5   1
Scale in kilometres

TRAIL 25: LIGHTNING LAKE LOOP

Distance:	9km return
Time:	2hrs 30mins
Rating:	easy
Base:	Vancouver or Hope
Map:	NTS 92H/2
Best Time:	July–September

Access
Start at Lightning Lake Day Use Area.

Trail Description

This trail follows the shoreline of the first of four lakes in the Lightning Lake Chain. There are several side-trails that lead closer to the lake. Part-way on the trail is a walking Gluelam bridge known as Rainbow Bridge. The eastern portion of the lake takes 1hr 30mins, and the western portion 1 hour. As you cross the bridge in a southern direction, there's an obvious beaver dam and, possibly, a beaver to be seen at the western end.

STEIN VALLEY NLAKA'PAMUX HERITAGE PARK

'Our tread has been deliberately light, but the spiritual and physical "footprints" of our peoples are evident for all to see throughout this watershed. To us, the valley is like the pages of a book upon which thousands of years of our history are written.'

'Our position, which will never waiver, is to maintain the forests of the Stein Valley in their natural state forever; to share our valley with other life forms equally; but also to share the valley with those people who can bring to the Stein, a respect for the natural life there similar to that taught us by our ancestors.'

– from the Stein Declaration, signed in 1987 by the Lytton and Mount Currie First Nations

History

In ancient times, the Stein Valley was one of the most densely populated places in the world. The ancient capital was Kumsheen, meaning 'Confluence of two great rivers'. Today Lytton is the centre for 11 contemporary Nlaka'pamux (pronounced ng-kla-KAP-muh), 'People of the canyon', communities. To the Nlaka'pamux who live there, the Stein is as significant as Rome is to Roman Catholics or Moses' Mountain to Christians and Jews. 'In the deep valleys of the dozens of rivers and creeks flowing into the Fraser is an unequalled source of spiritual sustenance.'

In the past, both allies and enemies shared the Stein Valley trail. In 1808, the Nlaka'pamux received the fur-trade explorer Simon Fraser on his quest down the present-named Fraser River. Having been led down the canyon at Hell's Gate, he would later write, 'we had to pass where no human being should venture'. Some 50 years of fur trading followed, and then in 1856 a Nlaka'pamux trader thought the glimmer of gold in the Thompson River might be worth something at the Hudson Bay Company's trading post at Fort Kamloops. For two years the Nlaka'pamux mined and sold their gold to the company, but then

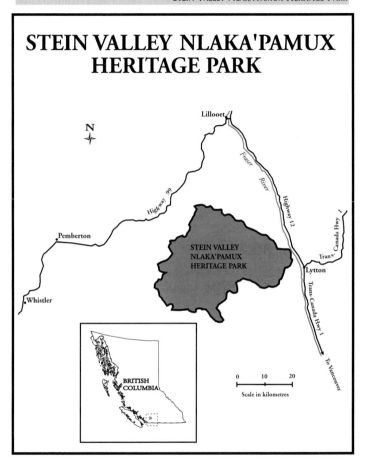

STEIN VALLEY NLAKA'PAMUX HERITAGE PARK

American miners found their way up the Fraser. The canyon people tried to block them, but the miners, trained on the American frontier, quickly learned that violence would get them through. What ensued was a full-scale war that ended up as a blood bath as more and more Americans arrived to annihilate the 'Indians'. In 1858, the colony of

British Columbia was declared, and settlers took over Nlaka'pamux land. New colonial policies were implemented to turn the canyon people into farmers, and the Nlaka'pamux were put in reserves located on rock or without legal access to water. Placer mines ate up salmon spawning beds and the salmon themselves were caught by commercial fisheries at the mouth of the Fraser River. Their ancient fishing rocks were dynamited to make room for roads and the Canadian Pacific Railway. In 1913, during construction of a second railway on the opposite riverbank, the canyon wall just above Hell's Gate slid down into the Fraser River. Upriver, people waited in anticipation of that year's major run of sockeye salmon. Meanwhile, at Hell's Gate, only a fraction of their long journey from the Pacific, millions of salmon battered themselves to death trying to reach their spawning grounds. In the years to come, only certain species of salmon could pass the new barrier when water levels were low enough. This is one of BC's biggest environmental disasters. Although fish ladders are helping now, salmon runs have never recovered from this.

The Stein Valley or 'hidden place' was unknown to the rest of the world until the 1970s, when the Nlaka'pamux and the St'a-t'imc who share it began to reveal its secrets. Shamans and young initiates seeking *xa'xa* – the power of nature – have left testimonies of their dreams and visions in red ochre in caves, on boulders and on cliffs. An important part of a young initiate's development was the quest for a guardian spirit. The initiate would travel to a peak or ledge above the river at dusk. He or she would light a fire and then sing and dance until dawn, when they would collapse from exhaustion. In the dreams that followed, the spirits that would protect and give the young person lifelong strength were revealed. The spirit, which would be a bird, animal or supernatural being, entered their dreams and spoke or sang. The song was very significant and would be used all through life to summon the spirit. One could then attain *xa'xa* and attain special attributes, such as great strength and endurance, immunity to danger and the ability to change into other forms. This would complete the youth's puberty rituals. The sacred pictographs make up one of the largest rock-art sites in Canada and also record the Nlaka'pamux's first experiences with white men, their supernatural beings and historic events. Many of these sacred artefacts and the traditional rock art are hidden in protected valleys and inaccessible caves known only to a few elders. Some of these pictographs record the 70-year war between the Nlaka'pamux and the St'a-t'imc that ended in 1850.

In 1985, after 135 years of peace, the two peoples joined together in a unified struggle to preserve the valley. By the late 1960s, logging of the valley had started, and by the 1980s it was apparent that the logging companies were overcutting. Environmentalists focussed on the ancient trails leading through old-growth forests. The first Voices for the Wilderness Festival, to raise awareness about the heritage about to be destroyed, brought together thousands from around the world. It's now called Earth Voice Festival and is held on Seabird Island in late July. In 1987, the Lytton and Mount Currie First Nations signed the Stein Declaration: a long-term vision as to what they wanted for the protected area over the next couple of centuries. In 1995, the entire 107,000 hectare valley was permanently protected as the Stein Valley Nlaka'pamux Heritage Provincial Park, to be managed co-operatively by the provincial government and the Lytton First Nation.

Getting There

The nearest town to the Stein Valley is Lytton. From Vancouver, drive on Highway 1 (TransCanada Highway) north. Lytton is between 1hr and 1hr 30mins north of Hope. From downtown Lytton at the junction of Main Street and 6th Avenue, it's 2km to the Lytton Ferry. Cross over the railway tracks, over a bridge that crosses the Thompson River and pass Botanie Valley Road on the right. Take a left off Highway 12 onto the Lytton Ferry access road. It's just under 1km further to the ferry. The ferry operates daily from 6.30am to 10.15pm, except for a few half-hour breaks. This ferry crosses the Fraser River. From the west side of the river, it's almost 5km to the Stein trailhead. After about 1.5km, you'll pass Earlscourt Farm on the left. There's a sharp bend in the road at 4km, and it's just a bit further to the trailhead turn-off. There is a parking area near the trailhead.

Camping in Lytton

Jade Springs Park (Open March–November) – 40 tent sites
Box 449
Lytton, BC
V0K 1Z0
Tel. (250) 455-6662

TRAIL 26: LOWER STEIN VALLEY

Distance:	28km one way
Time:	3–4 days return
Elevation change:	425m
Map:	NTS 92I/5
Rating:	moderate
Base:	Lytton or Vancouver
Best Time:	May–Oct

Background

The lower Stein Valley was called the 'Hidden place', and even after the Europeans came the valley remained untouched, in contrast to the other wilderness areas completely destroyed by chainsaws and bulldozers. In fact, this valley is the last major biologically complete unlogged valley in all of southwestern BC. The Stein Valley contains eight of the province's 14 major ecological zones: ponderosa pine bunchgrass semi-desert zones in the valley bottoms; five forest zones; and high alpine glacier zone above the tree line. This diversity supports populations of black bear, mountain goats, mule deer, moose, wolves, coyotes, marten, salmon, mink and beaver, and also provides the grizzly bear with its last refuge in southwest BC.

Trailhead to TeePee Site, 7.5km

The first 4km of the trail are fairly easy. From the parking area, the trail descends toward the river, crosses a bridge at Stryen Creek, and then goes over open, boulder-strewn pine flats leading eventually into a moister Douglas fir forest. The trail passes a campsite at 2km and another one just before the Devil's Staircase at 4km. There is a rougher, steeper section at Devil's Staircase. During the next 3.5km, there are two large talus-slope crossings. The first is about 300m long and ends with large boulders and a creek which floods over the trail in spring. The second is 200m long and ends at the Teepee Campsite. The campsite has a pit toilet and bear-proof cache. Please note that in the lower Stein Valley camping is only permitted at designated campsites.

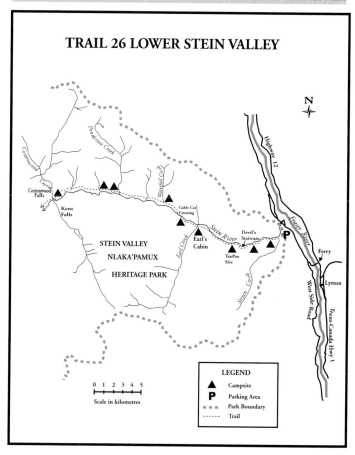

TRAIL 26 LOWER STEIN VALLEY

For hikers with limited time, this would make an ideal day-trip, being 15km long and about a 7 hours' round-trip.

TeePee Site to Waterfall Creek, 8km

The trail goes over rocky terrain through Douglas fir until Teaspoon Creek. The amount of vegetation increases to Earl's Cabin Campsite at 2.5km from the TeePee Site. At Teaspoon Creek, there are a number of cedar trees with large rectangular strips of bark missing. To the Nlaka'pamux, this area of cedars was an important source of fibre for clothing, baskets, rope, roofing and insulating materials. This area was so important that the Nlaka'pamux walked a 22km round-trip to collect it! There is a bridge made of two logs with a handrail crossing over Earl Creek. For the next 2km, the trail is easy and flat. At about the 12km, the trail is a rocky surface that follows closely the southern bank of the Stein River. Watch carefully for pictographs on the rock walls. There is a talus slope that requires careful footing and then an open clearing, before a creek is crossed. There is a cable crossing over the Stein River at 13km. Only one person can cross at a time. After the crossing, the trail heads 2.5km along the floodplains of the Stein River. Cross East Fickle, West Fickle and Shelter Creeks using the four logs as a bridge. There is a large campsite at Waterfall Creek Camp with a pit toilet and bear cache.

Waterfall Creek to Ponderosa Camp, 5.5km

In spring, the Stein River floodplain assists the ascent of Snake Bluffs. This area of the trail is rough and steep. Use caution when traversing the loose material covering the steep rocky sections of Snake Bluffs. After climbing back down to the floodplain, the wet area continues a further 300m. Walk at the foot of the hill and be careful. Fir and birch trees are prominent in this area. There are two crossings at Ponderosa Creek: one is a two-log crossing and the other is a single flattened log with a handrail. Just west of the creek crossing is the campsite at Ponderosa Camp.

Ponderosa Camp to Cottonwood Creek, 6km

From Ponderosa Camp, it is 2km on a flat trail through Douglas fir and cedar to Wrong Turn Camp, located at a tight bend in the river. Wrong Turn Camp is not a campsite. The next section of the trail is boggy and with thick vegetation. Just west of Swamp Bluffs, there is 300m of a talus slope to cross. There is a bridge made of four logs that crosses over Burnt Cabin Creek. The last section starts off rocky, then turns swampy, and then ends with an easy bit of trail. Take the south trail to Cottonwood crossing and campsite. There is a pit toilet and bear cache here. Look out for the tall black cottonwoods that give this area its name.

Emerald Lake in Yoho National Park (Trail 45)

Sunset over the west coast mountains (photo by Martijn Coini)

Rugged wilderness in northern British Columbia (photo by Martijn Coini)

Alternatives

The Stein Traverse

This is a hike that traces the Stein to its headwaters in the Coast Mountains. From the main trailhead to Lizzie Lake, it is a total length of 75km (allow 8–10 days). This hike is only for experienced and fit hikers, as once the halfway point is reached hikers are at least two days from help. Hikers must be proficient in wilderness survival and navigation. The trail starts in dry pine forest, goes into lush rich temperate rainforest and ends in a high alpine area with tundra and glaciers. For an update on trail conditions, contact: BC Parks, 1210 McGill Rd, Kamloops, V2C 6N6 or the Lytton Visitor InfoCentre, 400 Fraser St, Box 460, Lytton, BC V0K 1Z0. At the time of writing, this trail was not recommended because of the 25km mid-Stein section. A forest fire in 1996 had little effect on the trails, but there are a lot of blown-down trees, making the mid-Stein extremely difficult to traverse.

Day-use

The Stein Valley offers unlimited hiking opportunities from just a few hours to a full week or more. Even for those with limited time, it is well worth taking the drive to Lytton and the Stein Valley, even if just to get a glimpse of this special area.

MOUNT REVELSTOKE AND GLACIER NATIONAL PARKS

Natural History

In terms of natural history, Mount Revelstoke and Glacier can be considered as two parts of the same park, as they both preserve portions of the Columbia Mountain Natural Region in the interior of British Columbia. The Columbia Mountains are found west of the Rockies and are made up of the Purcells, Selkirks, Monashees and Cariboo Mountain ranges. The Columbias are an older mountain system than the Rockies, with sharp angular mountains, narrow steep-walled valleys, waterfalls, avalanche paths, icefields and glaciers. Most mountain systems start off jagged and are pared down by wind, rain and freeze-thaw conditions – the Columbias, however, resist erosion. Their steep mountain walls, large amounts of snow and near freezing or warmer temperatures combine to create ideal avalanche conditions. In Glacier National Park, avalanche slopes cover a large part of what would otherwise be forested areas. Tremendous amounts of snow have created many glaciers, and there are over 400 glaciers in Glacier National Park, covering 10% of its area. The only temperate inland rainforest in the world can be found in the Columbias. Here, old-growth moist to wet forests can be found, similar in both structure and composition to the rainforests found along BC's coasts. Rainforest conditions exist here as a result of abundant snowmelt during the early part of the growing season followed by lots of rain during the middle of the growing season. Humid conditions have led to the development of a unique vegetation community far inland that contains oceanic elements. The parks protect the dense old-growth cedar-hemlock stands. These stands represent a rapidly declining segment outside of the parks, and are vital habitat areas for threatened and endangered wildlife such as the Mountain caribou.

History

There is little known about the First Nations' use of the Columbia Mountains, but the Secwepemc peoples have lived in the area for

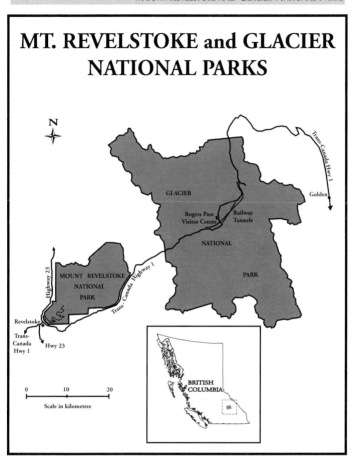

MT. REVELSTOKE and GLACIER NATIONAL PARKS

thousands of years. In recent history, white explorers of the fur trade and railway men feared this area of sharp mountain peaks scarred by unforgiving avalanches and perpetual ice. Before the railway, the confluence of the Columbia and Illecillewaet rivers just outside the boundaries of Mount Revelstoke National Park was used as a base camp by fur traders and explorers on the Columbia River and was a supply point for miners. In the late 1800s, there was much interest in finding a southern trade route through the western mountains to the Pacific Ocean. The ruggedness of the Columbia Mountains posed great problems. In 1881, Rogers Pass was discovered by Major AB Rogers, and construction on the Canadian Pacific Railway to complete the transcontinental railway continued. But avalanches and slides on this area of the track destroyed in seconds what it had taken years to build. The solution was to build the 9km Connaught Tunnel under the pass in 1916.

The site of Glacier House, the Canadian Pacific Railway hotel built in 1887 in present-day Glacier National Park, is the birthplace of mountaineering in North America. Swiss guides were hired by the railway company to introduce alpinism to the people and to lead first ascents of many of the local peaks from here. After the Connaught Tunnel was constructed the railway bypassed the hotel, and Glacier House was closed in 1925 and then demolished in 1929. Mount Revelstoke was used as one of Canada's first ski hills and a ski jump was built at the bottom. Many world records were set there before 1930.

Cultural Background

The Secwepemc (pronounced SHE-wep-m) people, also known as the Shuswap, are members of the Interior Salish First Nations. They have lived in the high plateau, the area between the Rockies in the east and the Coast Mountains in the west, for 8000–10,000 years according to archaeological evidence. The Secwepemc elders say their people have lived on this land for ever. In the past, the Secwepemc were a semi-nomadic people who based their lifestyle on a deep respect for nature, surviving in a land with very cold winters and very hot summers. In the summer they lived in mat lodges made of reeds, and in the winter they lived in semi-underground pit-houses or *kekuli*. A *kekuli*, which could hold 30 people, was built down into the ground, and the entrance and exit was through the smoke hole in the ceiling. A *kekuli* could keep people warm even when it was way below freezing outside. Secwepemc stories centre on Coyote, who was sent to put the world in order. Coyote sent helpers to bring peace into the world and taught the Secwepemc

View from the summit of Mount Revelstoke

people the rules of society. In the 19th century, their whole way of life was transformed by the arrival of fur traders, missionaries, gold miners and settlers. The smallpox epidemic in 1862, which effectively devastated whole populations of First Nations all over British Columbia, wiped out 32 Secwepemc villages. In 1871, the British Crown Colony of British Columbia agreed to become a province of Canada if the government built a railway north of the Great Lakes, across the plains and through the mountains to the Pacific coast. The federal Department of Indian Affairs assumed control over every aspect of the Secwepemc way of life and the lands that had always been their homes. Some of the Secwepemc horsemen and hunters became cowboys working for the big ranch owners. The Catholic Church was charged with the 'religious conversion' of the Secwepemc people, and residential schools were set up to 'westernize' their children. These schools existed into the 1970s and continue to be the focus of much controversy. The Secwepemc people have persevered, and they and their culture are very much alive; 17 bands representing 5000 people exist today.

Getting There

The city of Revelstoke is 410km west of Calgary and 575km east of Vancouver. Mount Revelstoke National Park is adjacent to the city, and the Rogers Pass Centre at Glacier National Park is only 72km east, making Revelstoke an ideal base for supplies and accommodation. Starting in Vancouver, take the TransCanada (Highway 1) towards Hope. From Hope, take the Coquihalla Highway (Highway 5) for a quick direct route to Kamloops, or continue on Highway 1 for the longer, slower route north through Lytton on to Kamloops. Both routes continue on Highway 1 from Kamloops to Revelstoke. Some 80km east of Glacier National Park is Golden, which also offers supplies, petrol and accommodation. From the south, Revelstoke is about a three-hour drive from Nelson. Use highway 3A to Balfour and then head towards Kaslo and Galena Bay on Highway 31. There is a half-hour free ferry from Galena Bay to Shelter Bay. A few kilometres before the ferry, stop off at Halcyon Hot Springs for a therapeutic soak surrounded by awe-inspiring alpine peaks. From Shelter Bay, follow Highway 23 north to Revelstoke.

Revelstoke Accommodation

Hostelling International
Revelstoke Traveller's Hostel and Guest House
400 Second Street, West
PO Box 1739
Revelstoke, BC
V0E 2S0
Tel: (250) 837-4050
Fax: (250) 837-6410

Completely renovated with seemingly endless numbers of kitchens and bathrooms! 24-hour check-in, bike rentals and complimentary guest internet and email are only some of the perks.

MOUNT REVELSTOKE NATIONAL PARK

Mount Revelstoke National Park is primarily a day-use park and protects more than 26,000 hectares of wilderness in the Monashee Mountains, including the 1830m summit of Mount Revelstoke. The area was established as a park in 1914 as a result of lobbying by the people of Revelstoke to protect the nearby mountain environment complete with its spectacular wildflower displays. The park is mostly dense forest, subalpine meadows and rushing streams, and includes more than 65km of hiking trails. It is a highly accessible park with a paved road leading to the summit of Mount Revelstoke with short trails leading to the meadows.

TRAIL 27: SUMMIT TRAIL

Distance:	**10km one way**
Time:	**4–5hrs one way**
Rating:	**moderate**
Elevation change:	**1230m**
Base:	**Revelstoke**
Map:	**NTS 82M/1**

Access
The lower trailhead is found at the edge of the parking area with the sign for trailer drop-offs at the base of Summit Road. The upper trailhead is beside the Balsam Lake warden cabin and parking area at the junction of Summit Road.

Trail Description
This trail, leading from the base of Mount Revelstoke up to the summit area, dates back to 1908 and was started by the city of Revelstoke. It was the first trail giving access to the now famous spectacular wildflower meadows of Mount Revelstoke. By 1927, there was a road leading up to the summit, giving easier access, but the trail has remained popular with hikers. On the way up, the trail crosses the

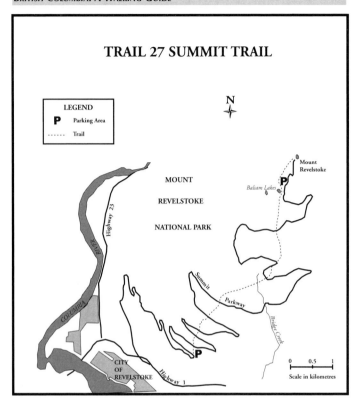

TRAIL 27 SUMMIT TRAIL

LEGEND

P Parking Area

------ Trail

N

MOUNT

REVELSTOKE

NATIONAL PARK

Mount Revelstoke

Balsam Lakes

P

Highway 23

COLUMBIA RIVER

Summit

Parkway

Bridge Creek

P

CITY OF REVELSTOKE

Highway 1

0   0.5   1

Scale in kilometres

road six times. At the seventh meeting, the trail joins the Summit Road for 1.2km. Keep on the lookout for trail signs on the left. The last part of the trail leads to the Balsam Lake warden cabin, where the trail ends. From here, hikers can choose the road to the summit or the trail to Balsam Lake. The trail begins in the Columbia forest and climbs through stands of western hemlock, western white pine and western red cedar. At 1300m Engelmann spruce, mountain hemlock and subalpine fir of the interior subalpine zone replace this forest. Near the end, by the Balsam Lake warden cabin, the subalpine forest gives away to meadows. In August, the meadows are painted with the sensational colours of blooming wildflowers: Indian paintbrush, mountain valerian, mountain daisies, lupine and arnica.

TRAIL 28: EVA LAKE TRAIL

Distance:	**6km one way**
Time:	**2hrs one way**
Rating:	**easy**
Elevation change:	**150m**
Base:	**Revelstoke**
Map:	**NTS 82M/1**

Eva Hobbs was an early explorer of Mount Revelstoke and an active member of the Revelstoke Mountaineering Club; this trail is named for her.

Access
The trailhead is located at the top of Summit Road on the eastern edge of the Heather Lake parking area.

Trail Description
From the trailhead, follow the signs to the junction with the Miller Lake and Jade Lakes trails, which is about 5.5km from the start. The trail goes through a transition zone between interior subalpine forest and the treeless alpine tundra. The trail crosses meadows that are carpeted with colourful wildflowers in late July and August. Turn left at the junction to go to Eva Lake. At Eva Lake, there is a small cabin that is open to the public and camping is permitted here. A short well-marked trail goes around the lake edge, and at the north end of the lake there is a spectacular view of the Coursier Creek Valley.

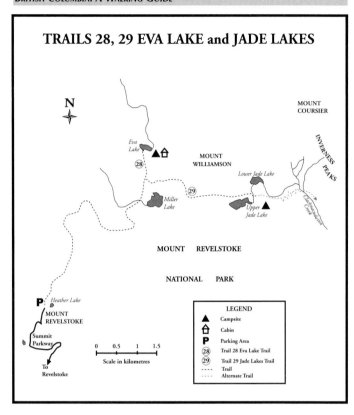

TRAILS 28, 29 EVA LAKE and JADE LAKES

N

Eva Lake

MOUNT COURSIER

MOUNT WILLIAMSON

INVERNESS PEAKS

(28)

Lower Jade Lake

Miller Lake

(29)

Upper Jade Lake

Lindmark Creek

MOUNT   REVELSTOKE

NATIONAL   PARK

P Heather Lake

MOUNT REVELSTOKE

Summit Parkway

To Revelstoke

LEGEND

▲ Campsite
⌂ Cabin
P Parking Area
(28) Trail 28 Eva Lake Trail
(29) Trail 29 Jade Lakes Trail
- - - - Trail
- - - - Alternate Trail

0   0.5   1   1.5
Scale in kilometres

TRAIL 29: JADE LAKES TRAIL

Distance:	9km one way
Time:	3hrs 30mins one way
Rating:	moderate
Elevation change:	425m
Base:	Revelstoke
Map:	NTS 82M/1

Access

The trailhead is located at the top of Summit Road on the eastern edge of the Heather Lake parking area.

Trail Description

The jade-green waters of these lakes have lured many a photographer with the strength to climb over the ridge separating Miller Lakes from Jade Lakes. The first 5.5km of the trail follows the same route as for Eva Lake. Follow the signs to the junction for Miller Lake and Jade Lakes. At the junction, follow the trail leading straight ahead. This trail ascends the steep ridge that separates Miller Lake from Jade Lakes. Near the summit of the pass, the trail enters the treeless alpine tundra that is home to the golden eagle, golden-mantled ground squirrel and hoary marmot. This is a great viewpoint for the mountains and valleys below. Very strong hikers may continue down the other side of the steep trail to Upper Jade Lake, where overnight camping is permitted.

TRAIL 30: GIANT CEDARS TRAIL

Distance:	**0.5km round trip**
Time:	**15–20mins**
Rating:	**easy**
Elevation change:	**minimal**
Map:	**NTS 82N/4**
Base:	**Revelstoke**

Access

On the TransCanada (Highway 1), drive east from Revelstoke. The trailhead is located across from the Giant Cedars picnic area on the north side of the road near the eastern boundary of Mount Revelstoke National Park.

Trail Description

A very short but worthwhile trail to do on the way to, or from, the longer trails. A boardwalk guides through the rainforest, with its huge

Giant Cedars in Mount Revelstoke National Park

TRAIL 30 GIANT CEDARS TRAIL

western red cedar trees that are typical of the wet valley-bottom forests of the Columbia Mountains.

GLACIER NATIONAL PARK

Glacier National Park, which protects parts of the Selkirks and the Purcells, was set aside in 1886 alongside Yoho National Park, and its history is intertwined with the early years of the Canadian Pacific Railway. Glaciers and rugged terrain have impeded trail construction in the park, and as a result most trails are short yet steep. Because of high elevation and deep snow pack, the hiking season is short in this area. Lower trails can be hiked May to November, but higher trails may only be snow-free from late July through September. During the winter, avalanches are a normal occurrence, but technology has progressed since the early days of the railway construction. The park can now predict fairly well when and where avalanches will occur, and is able to act before they happen. Seventeen circular emplacements were built along Rogers Pass, where 105-mm howitzer canons can be fired on avalanche danger spots. The potential avalanche is released before too much snow builds up, and the slide moves safely across one of the snow sheds that bridge the road, carrying the snow harmlessly further downslope.

Occasionally, a howitzer shell fails to explode on impact. All strange metal objects must be reported immediately to the park office. Do not touch it – it could blow up.

Registration at the park office is mandatory for all overnight trips, mountain climbing, glacier travel and all winter trips. You may also register for day-long hikes – and remember, if you register out, you **must**, by law, register back in. Hypothermia can be a serious concern in this area during all seasons – hikers should be prepared with extra clothing, raingear and food. Glacier National Park is remote wilderness and has a high population of both black bears and grizzly bears. The park protects critical habitats for both grizzly bears and mountain caribou.

Campgrounds
Illecillewaet Campground
Located 3km west of Rogers Pass
Open June–October
60 sites, a staffed welcome centre, tent pads, flush-toilet washroom buildings, log kitchen shelter, food lockers, free firewood, drinking water supplies

Loop Brook Campground
Located 5km west of Rogers Pass
Open June–October – self-serve check-in station near entrance
20 sites, tent pads, flush-toilet washroom buildings, log kitchen shelter, food lockers, free firewood, drinking water supplies

Mountain Creek Campground
250 sites

Alpine Huts
Asulkan Cabin
Located 6.5km up the Asulkan Brook, 300m from the end of the Asulkan Trail at 2100m
Can accommodate 12 people
Propane stove and heater, lights, loft and foam sleeping pads, eating utensils, cleaning supplies, toilet and grey water systems
Reservations can be made through the Alpine Club of Canada.

Wheeler Hut
Located at the south end of the Illecillewaet Campground.
A rustic hostel-style hut operated by the Alpine Club of Canada.
Well-furnished and completely equipped, sleeps 35-40 in the loft.
The Alpine Club of Canada manages two other huts in the area, Glacier Circle and Sapphire Col, which are accessible only to those with mountaineering experience.

Contact: Alpine Club of Canada
                PO Box 2040
                Canmore, Alberta
                T0L 0M0
                Tel. (403) 678-3200

Bookings can be made 30 days in advance.

TRAIL 31: ASULKAN VALLEY TRAIL

Distance:	**6.5km one way**
Time:	**4hrs uphill**
Rating:	**moderate–difficult**
Elevation change:	**925m**
Base:	**Revelstoke or Golden**
Maps:	**NTS 82N/6, 82N/3**

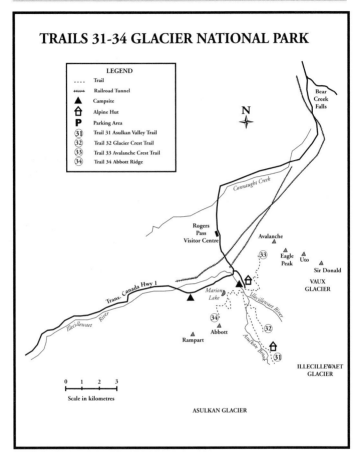

TRAILS 31-34 GLACIER NATIONAL PARK

LEGEND

- - - -	Trail
+++++	Railroad Tunnel
▲	Campsite
⌂	Alpine Hut
P	Parking Area
(31)	Trail 31 Asulkan Valley Trail
(32)	Trail 32 Glacier Crest Trail
(33)	Trail 33 Avalanche Crest Trail
(34)	Trail 34 Abbott Ridge

N

Bear Creek Falls

Connaught Creek

Rogers Pass Visitor Centre

Avalanche ▲

(33)

Eagle Peak ▲   Uto ▲

Sir Donald ▲

VAUX GLACIER

Trans-Canada Hwy 1

Illecillewaet River

Marion Lake

▲

⌂

Illecillewaet River

(34)   Abbott ▲

(32)

Rampart ▲

Asulkan Brook

⌂ (31)

ILLECILLEWAET GLACIER

0   1   2   3

Scale in kilometres

ASULKAN GLACIER

Access

Drive to the Illecillewaet Campground. Follow the hiker signs to the cabin behind the campground. Turn right and follow the road across the Illecillewaet River. The trailhead is obvious and is found ahead on the left beside the Glacier House sign.

Trail Description

This trail is best on a clear day. From the Glacier House sign, the trail gently rises, passing a number of junctions with other trails. Take care to follow the signs carefully and just stay right once past the Abbott Ridge junction. The route passes through different vegetation zones, and it is possible to see both western and mountain hemlock growing side by side. At 1.2km, a footbridge crosses Asulkan Brook before continuing up the Asulkan Valley bottom and across several avalanche paths. The mountains create an impressive backdrop, emphasized further by a number of waterfalls, and every so often the glaciers at the end of the valley appear. At about 4km, the trail begins a steep climb towards Asulkan Pass. A glacier-moulded moraine soon comes into view and then the Asulkan Glacier with its crevassed ice front. The trail ascends to a footbridge that crosses the upper reaches of Asulkan Brook. After passing through a small area of subalpine forest, the route begins a very steep ascent up the spine of another moraine before emerging in the alpine near the Asulkan Cabin and the Asulkan Glacier. The bare rock in front of the ice is where the glacier has retreated since its maximum extent in the Little Ice Age. The end of the trail is very near to the glacier, but only experienced and properly equipped hikers should attempt to walk on it. There are many dangerous crevasses on the glacier that are often hidden by a thin layer of snow.

TRAIL 32: GLACIER CREST TRAIL

Distance:	**4.8km one way**
Time:	**3hrs uphill**
Rating:	**moderate–difficult**
Elevation change:	**795m**
Base:	**Revelstoke or Golden**
Maps:	**NTS 82N/6, 82N/3**

Access

Drive to the Illecillewaet Campground. Follow the hiker signs to the cabin behind the campground. Turn right and follow the road across the Illecillewaet River. The trailhead is obvious and is found ahead on the left beside the Glacier House sign.

Trail Description
This trail offers glacier views on both sides: the giant tongue of Illecillewaet to the east and the walls of the Asulkan Glacier to the west. The ridge itself is an arête carved by glaciers that once flowed down the valleys on either side. Follow the signs from the trailhead. The trail climbs slowly through dense forest and then crosses Asulkan Brook before veering left. The trail then climbs continuously switch-backing. At the end, there is a great view of the Asulkan Brook valley. From here, many hikers choose their own routes to the summit of the crest. From the summit, the view is a Columbia Mountain panorama of rock and glacial ice.

TRAIL 33: AVALANCHE CREST TRAIL

Distance:	**4.2km one way**
Time:	**3hrs uphill**
Rating:	**moderate–difficult**
Elevation change:	**795m**
Base:	**Revelstoke or Golden**
Map:	**NTS 82N/6**
Best time:	**July–September**

This trail is known by local hikers as one of the most scenic trails in the park, offering unmatched views of Rogers Pass, the Illecillewaet Valley, the Asulkan Brook Valley, the Hermit Range and the Illecillewaet Neve. The treeless slopes stretching down the mountain are visible proof of the numerous avalanches that threaten every year from November to May.

Access
The trailhead is behind the Illecillewaet Campground. Follow the hiker signs to the Alpine Club of Canada cabin behind the campground. A major trailhead sign indicates the route.

Trail Description

After leaving the road, this trail branches off to the left. The trail passes through stands of old-growth western red cedar and huge Englemann spruce. The trail climbs, and at 1.6km a short side-trail leads off to a viewpoint of the Cascades, a waterfall that once supplied the Glacier House's fountain. Back on the main trail, the route climbs through open areas of the upper subalpine zone that bloom with colourful wildflowers. Don't take any of the old side-trails leading off to the right. Eagle Peak can be seen ahead and to the right; it is so named because from a distance it resembles the shape of an eagle. The trail winds its way onto and ends at Avalanche Crest.

TRAIL 34: ABBOTT RIDGE

Distance:	**5km one-way**
Time:	**4hrs uphill**
Rating:	**moderate–difficult**
Elevation change:	**1040m**
Base:	**Revelstoke or Golden**
Maps:	**NTS 82N/6, 82N/5, 82N/4**

This trail is named for Henry Abbott, one of the brave railway men of the early 1900s who dared to challenge these mountains. Abbott Ridge provides a view stretching from peak to peak while the railway still snakes below.

Access

Drive to the Illecillewaet Campground. Follow the hiker signs to the cabin behind the campground. Turn right and follow the road across the Illecillewaet River. The trailhead is obvious and is found ahead on the left beside the Glacier House sign.

Trail Description

The trail begins at the remains of Glacier House and then veers to the right as it follows the Marion Lake Trail up to the first junction. Take the right trail. The trail leaves the valley and continuously switchbacks up to the lake. The first hour is the steepest, but hikers are rewarded with Marion Lake and a good viewpoint from which to look out over Rogers Pass and the Illecillewaet Valley. At the fork, head left and follow the trail up above the lake. The trail comes to another junction. Hikers without ice axes should go right to avoid the incessant and dangerous snow patches often found on the main route. The trail climbs up towards the cliff base and becomes less apparent. The trail now enters the alpine zone and passes the Abbott Observatory. In winter, this observatory monitors snow-pack and weather conditions and provides the data necessary to analyse avalanche conditions. The white boxes contain weather-monitoring equipment, and the aluminum screen on the tower protects a precipitation gauge from fierce winds. The hut provides an emergency shelter for the researchers. The trail winds up onto the ridge, passing through alpine meadows to cliffs. From the cliff base, the trail twists north to the right and leads up a trail to the top of the ridge that offers amazing views.

Trail 35: Hermit Trail

Distance:	**2.8km one way**
Time:	**2hrs uphill**
Rating:	**difficult**
Elevation change:	770m
Base:	**Revelstoke or Golden**
Map:	NTS 82N/5

Access
The trailhead is located 1.5km north of the Glacier Park Lodge on the west side of the road.

Trail Description
This trail is short but a sheer test of strength, with an average grade of 27.5%, and has the local reputation of being the steepest trail in a park known for its steep trails. This trail has long been the access route for climbers into the Hermit Range, and from the end of the

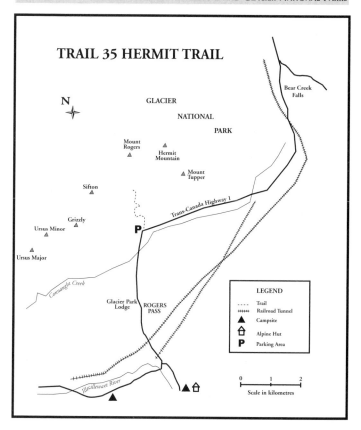

TRAIL 35 HERMIT TRAIL

GLACIER

NATIONAL

PARK

Bear Creek
Falls

N

Mount
Rogers

Hermit
Mountain

Mount
Tupper

Sifton

Trans-Canada Highway 1

Grizzly

P

Ursus Minor

Ursus Major

Connaught Creek

Glacier Park
Lodge

ROGERS
PASS

LEGEND

-----	Trail
++++++	Railroad Tunnel
▲	Campsite
⌂	Alpine Hut
P	Parking Area

Illecillewaet River

▲ ⌂

▲

0   1   2

Scale in kilometres

trail climbers can scale Mount Tupper, Mount Rogers or Hermit
Mountain. The trail begins at the Hermit parking area and then enters
dense interior subalpine forest. It ends in Hermit meadows. From
these alpine meadows, there are great views of Rogers Pass area –
the angular peaks of the Selkirks contrasting with the rounded
Purcells. The Asulkan Valley can be seen in the distance beyond
Rogers Pass.

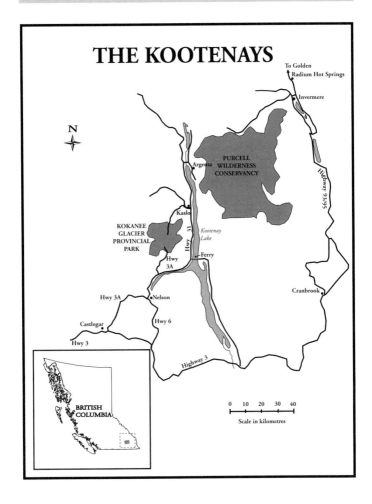

THE KOOTENAYS

To Golden
Radium Hot Springs

Invermere

N

Highway 93/95

PURCELL
WILDERNESS
CONSERVANCY

Argenta

Kaslo

Kootenay
Lake

KOKANEE
GLACIER
PROVINCIAL
PARK

Hwy 31

Ferry

Hwy
3A

Cranbrook

Hwy 3A

Nelson

Castlegar

Hwy 6

Hwy 3

Highway 3

0   10   20   30   40

Scale in kilometres

BRITISH
COLUMBIA

THE KOOTENAYS

Natural History
The Kootenays stretch from the Monashee Mountains in the west to the Purcell Mountains in the east. It's a region of snow-capped peaks, forested valleys and large inland lakes, with long hot, dry summers and cold and dry winters. Both wildlife and people thrive in this region: the towns have a distinct relaxed, good-natured ambience, and the wilderness regions are teeming with deer, moose, caribou, elk, bighorn sheep, mountain goats, black and grizzly bears, bald eagles and golden eagles.

Getting There
Nelson is 640km from Vancouver and 630km from Calgary. From Vancouver, a good scenic drive is through the Okanagan. Take the TransCanada Highway (Highway 1) to Hope and then take Highway 3 through Manning Park to Osoyoos to Castlegar. From Castlegar, take Highway 3A north to Nelson.

Nelson Accommodation
Dancing Bear Inn
171 Baker Street
Nelson, BC
V1L 4H1
Tel: (250) 352-7573
Fax: (250) 352-9818
www.dancingbearinn.com

Offers both shared and private accommodation, a common room with a library of books, games and movies, kitchen and laundry facilities, and internet access. Wake up to soothing new-age music – a great atmosphere with original art and furnishings by local artisans. The Dancing Bear Inn was voted one of the best hostels on the continent by Independent Hostellers Guide.

   Nelson is a very laid-back and friendly bohemian/snowboarder town with a population of about 9000. There are little cafes, bookshops and art galleries to explore. Cottonwood Falls Park, which has a gushing, powerful waterfall, is home of the Tree of Life Market on Saturdays from 9am–2pm with artisans' products, food and jewellery.

Trail 36: Pulpit Rock Hike

Distance:	1km
Time:	1hr
Rating:	moderate
Elevation change:	200m
Map:	NTS 82F/11
Base:	Nelson

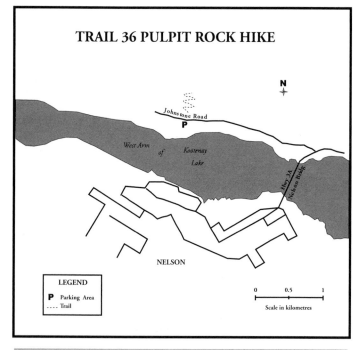

Access
The trailhead is located on the north shore of Nelson across the orange bridge. Across the bridge, take Johnstone Road 2km to the dirt pull-out on the left.

Trail Description
This is a great short hike that affords amazing views of Nelson and its surroundings. From the dirt pull-out, walk 50m along the road and then hike up the very steep and rough 4-wheel-drive road about 100m. The trail heads straight up Elephant Mountain (Mount Nelson) from the road and eases after the power lines. It is a steep climb, but the views of the west arm of Kootenay Lake, Nelson and the forested mountains to the south are well worth the effort.

KOKANEE GLACIER PROVINCIAL PARK

Background
Kokanee Glacier Provincial Park was established in 1922 and protects 32,000 hectares of the Slocan Range of the Selkirk Mountains: an area of glaciers, mountain peaks, alpine meadows, waterfalls and more than 30 glacial lakes. Most of the park lies above 1800m. It is one of the oldest parks in the province and contains three glaciers: Kokanee, Caribou and Woodbury. Kokanee is a Kootenai word meaning 'red fish', referring to the land-locked salmon of Kootenay Lake. Geologically, the park is composed of a massive system of granite known as the Nelson batholith. During the earth's cooling process, slower-cooling mineralized solutions were subjected to great pressure that caused them to be pushed into holes and cracks in the granite. These became the mineral deposits, rich in gold and silver ore, which caused the local mining boom in the late 1800s. Many of the trails in the park were first built for miners hauling ore and supplies.

The park includes many steep slopes and avalanche paths, but also lower forested slopes of Engelmann spruce, alpine fir, lodgepole pine, hemlock, western red cedar and alpine larch. Kokanee Glacier Provincial Park contains most of the range for several grizzly bears. In 1995, the park expanded to further protect grizzly bear habitat. In order to do so, places like Coffee Creek have no development and use of the area is discouraged. Other trails in the park have been carefully designed to avoid bear habitat or are closed at certain times of the year when bears are feeding on the berries nearby.

Alpine Cabins
There are three alpine cabins within the park and all are operated on a first-come-first-served basis, so it is wise to bring camping equipment just in case during the busy months of July and August.

Slocan Chief Cabin
Facilities: Sleeps 12; has sleeping pads, propane heat, lights, and cooking facilities.

Woodbury Cabin
Sleeps 6

Silver Spray Cabin
Sleeps 8

TRAIL 37: GIBSON LAKE TO SLOCAN CHIEF CABIN

Distance:	9km
Time:	4hrs 30mins one way
Rating:	moderate
Elevation change:	457m
Map:	NTS 82F/11, 82F/14
Base:	Nelson
Best time:	July–early October

Access
From Nelson, drive 19.2km north on Highway 3A to the sign for Kokanee Creek Park. At all the junctions, follow the well-marked signs. It is 16km along a gravel road to the Gibson Lake parking area. The trailhead is at the parking area, and there is detailed information about the area and the trail.

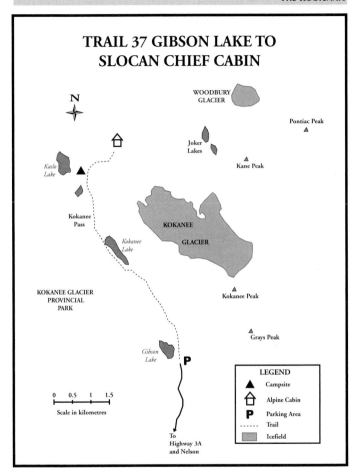

TRAIL 37 GIBSON LAKE TO SLOCAN CHIEF CABIN

N

WOODBURY GLACIER

Pontiac Peak
▲

Joker Lakes

Kane Peak
▲

Kaslo Lake
▲

Kokanee Pass

KOKANEE GLACIER

Kokanee Lake

Kokanee Peak
▲

KOKANEE GLACIER PROVINCIAL PARK

Grays Peak
▲

Gibson Lake
P

LEGEND

▲ Campsite

⌂ Alpine Cabin

P Parking Area

- - - - - Trail

▨ Icefield

0   0.5   1   1.5
Scale in kilometres

To Highway 3A and Nelson

Trail Description

This is one of the most popular hikes in the West Kootenays, known for its great scenery. The first part of the trail is steep, as the route steadily switchbacks through the dense forest. But after this first section, the trail leaves the forest and opens to the mountains, crossing large avalanche paths. The trail continues over a bridge and along the side of Kokanee Lake. It is about 4.4km and 2 hours from the beginning to the lake. Kokanee Lake is the largest lake in Kokanee Glacier Provincial Park, a crystal-blue subalpine basin great for fishing. Look out for marmots and pikas along the water's edge. From Kokanee Lake to Kaslo Lake is an easy 3km (1hr 30mins) descent into alpine meadows. Kaslo Lake is a good place to camp and has eight tent pads, an out-house, bear-proof cache and grey water pit. For hikers continuing on to the Slocan Chief Cabin, the trail climbs for the last 2km (1 hour) with great glacier views. The Slocan Chief Cabin is a 100-year-old structure that was almost destroyed in a forest fire in the 1930s. It was saved by a number of citizens who rode in to create a firebreak to save the cabin and its surrounding green space. In doing so, they created a temporary refuge for wildlife from the area. The cabin cannot be pre-booked, but if it is full there are also 11 tent pads, an out-house and a bear-proof cache. For experienced and well-equipped mountaineers, several peaks can be reached from the Slocan Chief Cabin.

PURCELL WILDERNESS CONSERVANCY

Background
The Purcell Wilderness Conservancy was created in 1974 and included 131,500 hectares of the Purcell Mountains and most of the Earl Grey Pass Trail. Recent expansions have increased the size to 199,683 hectares. The area protects prime grizzly bear habitat. In the past environmentalists have battled against development – there was a major controversy over a ski resort to be built below Jumbo Pass, and many bumperstickers in evidence saying 'Grizzlies not Gondolas.'

TRAIL 38: EARL GREY PASS TRAIL

Distance:	**61km**
Time:	**5–7 days**
Rating:	**difficult**
Elevation change:	**975m**
Map:	**NTS 82K/SE**
Base:	**Radium Hot Springs or Nelson**
Best time:	**July–September**

History

This trail was well established by the Shuswap people by the time Earl Grey arrived in 1908. It crossed the Purcell Mountains to Kootenay Lake, climbing up Toby Creek and down Hamil Creek over a 2256m pass. Kinbasket, a member of the Shuswap band, is believed to have led people over this route in the early 1800s to establish their present home near Invermere. During the late 1800s and early 1900s, the trail was an important access and supply route from the east, and cattle were even driven over the pass from Invermere. In 1908, Earl Grey, who was Canada's Governor-General of the day, travelled the trail on horseback and by foot. He was so impressed by the Purcell Mountains that he tried to get the area designated as a national park – but was unsuccessful. But he did have a cabin built for his family's vacation in 1909, and the structure still stands today, 3km from the eastern trailhead.

Access

The Toby Creek trailhead is located at the eastern end of the trail. From here, it is easy to do either the whole trail or a day-hike. From Radium Hot Springs, take Highway 95 south to the town of Invermere. Follow the signs from Invermere towards the Panorama ski resort. The resort is located on the Toby Creek Road about 15 minutes from Invermere. Stay on the Toby Creek Road and don't exit left for the ski resort. The paved road soon changes to a rougher gravel road and the trailhead is 20km further. Immediately before the trailhead, there is a fork in the road with a signpost between the roads. Stay left to carry on to the

TRAIL 38 EARL GREY PASS TRAIL

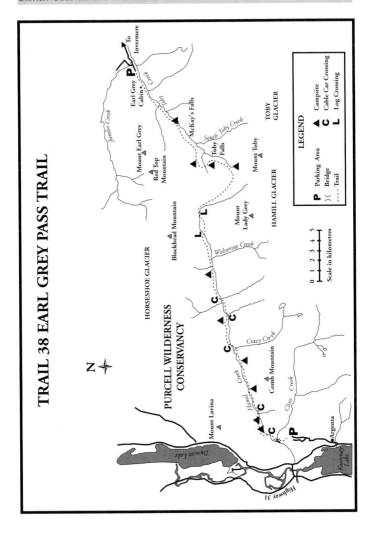

LEGEND

P Parking Area
)(Bridge
- - - Trail
▲ Campsite
C Cable Car Crossing
L Log Crossing

0 1 2 3 4 5
Scale in kilometres

Corral. The western trailhead is near the town of Argenta. To get to Argenta, drive north from Nelson on Highway 3A and then follow Highway 31 past Kaslo until the turn-off for Argenta. Follow the main road through Argenta just beyond the post office to reach the trailhead.

If shuttling cars between the eastern and western trailheads, allow a whole day as it is about 7 hours of driving between the two.

Trail Description

The Earl Grey Pass Trail is a 61km trail extending over the Purcell Mountains. From the eastern trailhead at Toby Creek, the trail leads over the slopes of the Toby Creek Valley, over the Earl Grey Pass and down Hamill Creek. There are great views of peaks, glaciers and waterfalls. The trail leads through old-growth cedar-hemlock forest, and has many cable-car crossings and log bridge crossings. This hike is a true wilderness experience and should only be attempted by experienced and well-equipped hikers. The trail goes through densely vegetated avalanche paths and sometimes may be difficult to locate, so a compass and topographical map are absolutely necessary. Bears may be encountered at any time, so always be alert. Check in with BC Parks in Nelson for up-to-date trail conditions or call (604) 825-4421.

Alternatives

A good day-hike leads to into the upper valley and to a view of Toby Falls. There is good two- or three-day trip to the outwash plain of the Toby Glacier.

TRAIL 39: LAKE OF THE HANGING GLACIER RECREATION TRAIL

Distance:	**8km**
Time:	**2hrs 30mins – 3 hours one way**
Rating:	**moderate**
Elevation change:	**700m**
Map:	**NTS 82K/7**
Base:	**Invermere or Radium Hot Springs**
Best time:	**July–September**

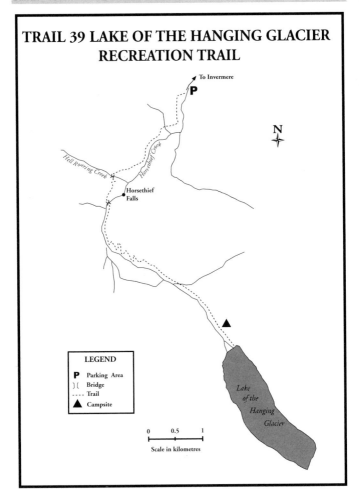

TRAIL 39 LAKE OF THE HANGING GLACIER RECREATION TRAIL

To Invermere

P

Hell Roaring Creek

Horsethief Creek

Horsethief Falls

N

Lake of the Hanging Glacier

LEGEND

P   Parking Area

)(Bridge

-----   Trail

▲   Campsite

0   0.5   1

Scale in kilometres

Access

Access to the trail is via the Horsethief Creek Forest Service Road. From Invermere, drive north to Wilmer and continue on the Westside

Subalpine meadow on the trail from Garibaldi Lake to Black Tusk (Trail 18)

(photo by Jonathan Deakin)

Trail to Black Tusk summit at 7600ft – Trail 18 (photo by Jonathan Deakin)

Garibaldi Park from Black Tusk – Trail 18 (photo by Jonathan Deakin)

Road for 16.4km to its junction with the Horsethief Creek Forest Service Road. From Radium, at the Highway 93/95 junction, drive west past the sawmill. Continue on the Horsethief Creek Forest Service Road to its end (km50 mark) for trailhead parking. There is an out-house at the trailhead. Overnight camping is permitted at the Stockdale Creek Forest Service Recreation Site at the km39 mark.

Trail Description

The trail follows an old railway route for the first 2km and then narrows. A footbridge has been installed to cross over Hell Roaring Creek, but please note that the footbridge is only there from July to September, and crossing when the bridge is not there may be treacherous! A second bridge crosses over Horsethief Creek, named for the two cattle rustlers who were apprehended in the creek's lower reaches in the 1880s. They were taken to Fort Steele and hanged. Prior to the bridge being built, the wild torrent had killed many people. The route then climbs through mature forest in a series of 13 moderate switchbacks. There is a detour above a small slough where the trail gently climbs to alpine meadows. Open camping and an out-house toilet are available here. The trail ends at the lake a further 800m through open meadows. Many agree that this area is one of the most beautiful places in the country. The tongue of the glacier is 2.5km from the lake's north shore, and an awe-inspiring panorama of peaks encircle the lake. Camping and fires are not permitted near the lakeshore. It is possible to get near to the glacier on the eastern shore. There are no trails over the rocky terrain; use caution. Only experienced and well-equipped hikers should attempt any travel on the glacier.

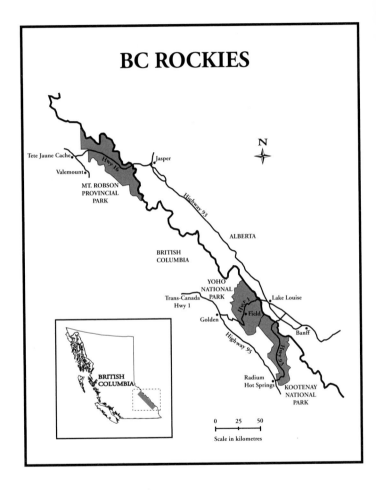

BC ROCKIES

N

Tete Jaune Cache
Valemount
Hwy 16
MT. ROBSON
PROVINCIAL
PARK

Jasper

Highway 93

ALBERTA

BRITISH
COLUMBIA

YOHO
NATIONAL
PARK

Trans-Canada
Hwy 1

Hwy 1

Lake Louise

Golden

Field

Banff

Highway 95

Radium
Hot Springs

Hwy 93

KOOTENAY
NATIONAL
PARK

BRITISH
COLUMBIA

0   25   50

Scale in kilometres

THE BC ROCKIES

'People sometimes accuse me of being a mystic about the influences of the mountains. Perhaps I am. I devoutly believe that there are emanations from them, intangible but very real, which elevate the mind and purify the spirit.' – JB Harkin, Parks Commissioner, 1911–36

Natural History

BC's Rocky Mountains are one of the easternmost ranges of the Canadian Cordillera, the huge belt of mountains that extends from the Interior Plains in the east to the Pacific Ocean in the west. The peaks range in altitude from 1036m to 3954m. The BC Rockies have been designated as a UNESCO world heritage site in recognition of the area's outstanding natural beauty and biodiversity. Three life zones are represented here: montane, subalpine and alpine. The montane zone covers the valley bottoms and sun-exposed slopes of the lower mountains. The subalpine zone is the most extensive region, between 1800m and 2100m, and the valley bottoms at high elevations. The dominant species of the subalpine forest are Engelmann spruce, lodgepole pine, limber pine and subalpine fir. The alpine zone covers the area above the treeline. The BC Rockies boast over 280 bird species and 56 mammalian species, including bighorn sheep, Rocky Mountain goat, moose, deer, caribou, grey wolf, grizzly bear, black bear, wolverine, lynx and puma.

Background

The Ktunaxa (pronounced Tun-AH-hah) people, also known as Kutenai, Kootenai and Kootenay, have lived here for at least 14,000 years. Their traditional territory is extensive, stretching from south-eastern British Columbia down to Montana and Idaho. In the area between four parallel mountain ranges, the Rockies, Purcells, Selkirks and Monashees, the Ktunaxa communities flourished in isolation for thousands of years. Their language, like the Haida language, is an isolate, in that it is not related to any other. In the 7500 years following the ice age, the Ktunaxa lived mainly in what used to be the dry, open forests of the Purcell Mountains. The communities on the wetter west side travelled by canoe on the lakes and rivers and mainly fished for their food or hunted small game. The people who lived on the drier east side hunted bison and large prehistoric animals. Some would cross the Rockies to hunt bison and then return again. The Ktunaxa people survived floods, earthquakes and little ice ages. The Kinbasket Shuswap are a group of Shuswap-speaking people who are closely aligned with the Ktunaxa and have lived in the area since at least the 19th century. They descend from the North Thompson Shuswap, a group of Shuswap who lived an almost completely nomadic existence and spent their winters in the Columbia Valley between Golden and Windermere. They are called Kinbasket, or the Children of Kinbasket, after one of the great Shuswap men who brought his people here in the 1800s.

It was in 1807 that the first white fur trader, David Thompson, came to the area. The Ktunaxa helped him to set up the region's first trading post on Lake Windermere. After Thompson, it was the gold-seekers and miners who came blasting their way through the mountain walls. Within 50 years smallpox hit, wiping out many communities. And then in 1846, north and south were divided by an invisible international boundary. By 1887, the Indian Act was imposed in Canada and the semi-nomadic Ktunaxa were forced into reserves. The Columbia and Kootenay rivers were dammed from head to mouth. Today, the Ktunaxa are ever present; they resist the international boundary and strive to hold onto their culture, their language and their tradition. They have initiated the Canadian Columbia River Intertribal Fisheries Commission to restore salmon to their rivers. The Ktunaxa Ethnobotany Project was started in 1996 in an attempt to document the traditional uses and names for all the plants and the places where they were gathered, and to produce educational materials to be used by both present and future generations. There is a sense of urgency, as much of their tradition and ancient knowledge lies with the elders, who are dying off. Since its start, the goals of the project have expanded to include resource protection, land management, education, oral history and economic development.

Climate

Weather in the BC Rockies can vary considerably from one part of a park to another, and from the valley bottoms to the tops of the moun-

Marble Canyon – Kootenay National Park

tains. The weather can be unpredictable and change dramatically in any short period of time. Temperatures can vary from -30°C in the winter to +30°C in the summer, and above 1500m snow and freezing temperatures can occur at any time during the summer. Generally, the Rockies have a continental cool summer and subarctic conditions, with the valleys being about 5–7 degrees warmer than higher elevations.

Note: The Rocky Mountain Parks are on Mountain Time, which is 1 hour ahead of Pacific Time (and most of British Columbia).

Getting There
Kootenay National Park
Kootenay National Park is 888km east of Vancouver and 260km west of Calgary, and can be reached from the south via Highway 93/95 or from the north via the TransCanada (Highway 1) at Castle Junction in Banff National Park (take Highway 93 – the Kootenay Parkway – south) or from Golden via Highway 95.
Yoho National Park
The town of Field and Yoho National Park are 205km east of Revelstoke, 771km east of Vancouver, 213km west of Calgary, 57km east of Golden and 85km west of Banff. The TransCanada Highway (Highway 1) runs directly through the park.
Mount Robson Provincial Park
Mount Robson Provincial Park lies just west of Jasper National Park and the BC/Alberta border. It is 5 hours west of Edmonton via Highway 16, 3hrs 30mins east of Prince George via Highway 16, and 4 hours north of Kamloops via Highway 5.

Yoho, Banff, and Jasper are all accessible by rail and bus.

Getting Around
Brewster – coach service

www.brewster.ca

tel. 1-800-661-1152

   (403) 762-6700

Hostelling International Alberta operates a daily shuttle service from

June to September from Calgary, Banff, Lake Louise and Jasper, stopping at all the hostels along the way. Enquire at any of the hostels.

Driving Distances

Vancouver to Radium Hot Springs	818km
Vancouver to Yoho National Park	771km
Calgary to Lake Louise	186km
Revelstoke to Lake Louise	224km
Radium Hot Springs to Lake Louise	157km
Golden to Field (Yoho National Park)	49km
Lake Louise to Jasper	233km

Accommodation
Radium Hot Springs
Misty River Lodge
5036 Highway 93, Box 363
Radium Hot Springs, BC
V0A 1M0
Tel. (250) 347-9912
Fax (250) 347-9397
Email: geoffi@rockies.net

Offers hostel and B&B accommodation, kitchen facilities, BBQ and bicycle storage.

Yoho National Park
Whiskey Jack Hostel
(operated by Hostelling International Southern Alberta)
Box 1358, Banff, Alberta
T0L 0C0
Tel. (403) 762-4122
Fax (403) 762-3441

Closed: October – mid-June
Located near Takakkaw Falls within Yoho National Park.
Directions: 13km west on the Yoho Valley Road from Kicking Horse Campground.

Lake Louise, Alberta
Canadian Alpine Centre and International Hostel
Box 115
Lake Louise, Alberta
T0L 1E0
Tel. (403) 522-2200
Fax (403) 522-2253

Large hostel that can accommodate 150 people in various types of rooms. Facilities include a mountaineering library, on-site cafe, laundry facilities, ski/bike workshops, sauna and games room.

Jasper, Alberta
Jasper International Hostel
Box 387
Jasper, Alberta
T0E 1E0
Tel. (780) 852-3215 or 1-877-852-0781
Fax (780) 852-5560

Located 7km southwest of Jasper on Whistler's Mountain Road (Skytram Road), off Highway 93, 0.5km below the Skytram parking area.

Wilderness Passes
All visitors staying overnight in the backcountry must have a valid wilderness pass. The wilderness pass fee is valid for Kootenay, Yoho, Banff, Jasper, Waterton, Mount Revelstoke and Glacier national parks, and is charged per person per night to a maximum per trip. An annual pass is available for purchase, but campers must register each trip.

Visitors wanting to stay overnight in the backcountry at Kootenay National Park must reserve their campsite; reservations can be made up to three months in advance. From mid-June to October, reserve at the Kootenay National Park Information Centre (tel. (250) 347-9505 or fax (250) 347-6307); off-season reservations can be made through the Lake Louise Visitors' Centre (tel. (403) 522-3833 or fax (403) 522-1212).

Voluntary Registration

Hikers may register at the Warden Office or at a Parks Canada Information Centre. Registration means that if a person does not return by their due date, Parks Canada will initiate a search-and-rescue effort. Anyone who registers **must**, by law, also register his or her return.

KOOTENAY NATIONAL PARK

Background

Kootenay National Park was established in 1920 and contains 1406km² of the west side of the Rockies, sloping down to the Rocky Mountain Trench, a valley that separates the Rockies from the Columbia Mountains in the Interior. The park signifies the best representation of the Western Ranges of the Rockies, characterized by overturned folds, a feature unique in the Rockies. They are composed of soft shale with some limestone beds – craggy, serrated ridges alternate with rounded, smooth crests. The landscape of the park is very different from north to south, and it is the only park that contains both glacial peaks and cactus! The south is a much drier area, the air currents having already dispersed their moisture over the Columbias, but the north is moist and contains three river valleys and wetter forest species.

Radium Hot Springs

Radium Hot Springs have been a source of spiritual cleansing for thousands of years, and the mineral waters are known for their therapeutic and medicinal value. Algae and microscopic plants often give the waters their spectacular colour – sometimes a deep emerald green and sometimes a milky sapphire blue. Radium Hot Springs have been diverted into two pools: the hot pool is 40°C (103°F), and the cool pool is 27°C (80°F). The pools are open all year, the cafe is open May through October, and facilities include towel and swimsuit rental, changing rooms, showers and coin-operated lockers.

Campgrounds

Campsites are available on a first-come, first-served basis only.

Hector Gorge – Kootenay National Park

Redstreak Campground
Located 2.5km from Radium Hot Springs
242 sites
Open May–October
Facilities: flush toilets, showers, kitchen shelters, firewood, telephone,
piped water, food storage bin for cyclists

McLeod Meadows Campground
Located 27km north of the West Gate entrance
98 sites
Open mid-May – mid-September
Facilities: flush toilets, firewood, piped water, kitchen shelters, food
storage bin for cyclists

Marble Canyon Campground
Located 86km north of the West Gate entrance or 7km south of the
Banff/Kootenay boundary
61 sites

Open mid-June–September
Facilities: flush toilets, kitchen shelters, firewood, piped water, food storage for cyclists

TRAIL 40: ROCKWALL TRAIL

Distance:	**55km**
Time:	**4–5 days**
Rating:	**moderate–difficult**
Elevation change:	**760m**
Map:	**NTS 82N/1**
Base:	**Radium Hot Springs or Lake Louise**
Best time:	**July–September**

The Rockwall is the name given to the Ottertail limestone cliff that extends 53km through parts of both Kootenay and Yoho national parks. This long-distance trail is a premier hike, with high mountain peaks, glaciers, passes, valleys and meadows. Note that water is scarce on the trail and hikers should refill their water supplies when it is available.

Access
The Floe Lake trailhead is located on the west side of Highway 93, 32.6km west of Castle Junction and 72km from Radium Hot Springs.

Trail Description
Trailhead to Floe Lake Campground, 10.5km
From the Floe Lake parking area, the trail descends and crosses over the Vermillion River. The river's name comes from its red banks upstream, stained by iron oxides. The trail is fairly flat as it follows the river northwest towards Floe Creek. The creek is crossed via a suspension bridge. The lower valley of Floe Creek is lush with Douglas fir and devil's club. Huge Engelmann spruce trees fill the upper valley. The trail crosses several south-facing avalanche paths; the vegetation on these slopes provides food for moose, elk, deer and

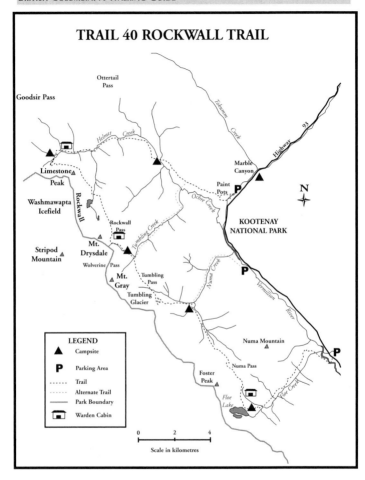

TRAIL 40 ROCKWALL TRAIL

Ottertail
Pass

Goodsir Pass

Helmet Creek

Tokumm Creek

Highway 93

Marble
Canyon

Paint
Pots

P

Limestone
Peak

Washmawapta
Icefield

Rockwall

Ochre Creek

N

Rockwall
Pass

Tumbling Creek

KOOTENAY
NATIONAL PARK

Stripod
Mountain

Mt.
Drysdale

Wolverine Pass

P

Mt.
Gray

Tumbling
Pass

Numa Creek

Vermilion River

Tumbling
Glacier

P

Numa Mountain

LEGEND

▲   Campsite

P   Parking Area

- - - -   Trail

········   Alternate Trail

———   Park Boundary

🏠   Warden Cabin

Numa Pass

Foster
Peak

Floe Creek

*Floe
Lake*

P

0   2   4

Scale in kilometres

bears, so be on the alert and make noise. At 8km, the trail reaches the valley headwall and begins climbing. In the next 2.5km, the trail climbs 400m. Just before the Floe Creek Campground, the forest changes to an upper subalpine forest of mainly Lyall's larch. Floe Lake is an idyllic setting, with the great Rockwall as a backdrop and views of glacier, mountain and meadow. The lake is named for the ice floes that calve from the glacier beneath the Rockwall. The campground has 18 tent sites and two pit toilets. Bring a stove, as fires are not permitted.

Floe Lake Campground to Numa Creek Campground, 9.5km

From the campground, the trail crosses over to the Warden Cabin and then ascends steeply to Numa Pass. The trail winds up through the upper subalpine larch forest with spectacular wildflower displays. Peak bloom is in early August. The last kilometre to Numa Pass is through alpine tundra. Continuous freeze-thaw conditions have churned the soil into mounds called frost hummocks. Numa is a Cree word for thunder, and Numa Mountain was first known as 'Roaring mountain'. From Numa Pass, Mount Temple (3543m) and the Wenkchemna Peaks can be seen to the north, and Foster Peak (3204m) to the west. From Numa Pass, the trail continues west on a route worn into screes and then descends north to the treeline. The trail descends steeply to the Numa Creek Campground, 840m in 6.8km. The trail passes through lush vegetation at the edge of avalanche paths – prime bear habitat. The trail crosses over Numa Creek on a bridge made from a felled tree. The bridge can be extremely slippery when wet. The Numa Creek Campground has 18 tent sites scattered on both sides of a stream. There is a pit toilet and firewood.

Numa Creek Campground to Tumbling Creek Campground, 7.9km

Just past the campground is the first exit point from the Rockwall Trail. The trail straight ahead follows Numa Creek 6.4km back to Highway 93. For those continuing on, take the trail to the left to climb up to Tumbling Pass. These avalanche slopes are prime bear-feeding spots during berry season. The trail continuously switchbacks up the course of a glacial stream. The mountain to the east is Mount Ball (3311m). The trail fords several small streams as it ascends. Finally, the trail levels out through 1km of alpine meadow. Numa Pass can be seen to the south. At the north end of the meadow the trail climbs steeply, detouring around a lateral moraine, over the scree shoulder east of Tumbling Pass. The climb is worth it, and from Tumbling Pass there are fantastic views of Tumbling Glacier. The trail descends along the side of a lateral moraine with forest to the east and barren land of rock to the west. At the north end of the lateral moraine, the trail heads northeast and descends steeply to Tumbling Creek. Hikers who wish to exit the trail at this point can follow Tumbling Creek and Ochre Creek trails 11km back to Highway 93. The Tumbling Creek Campground is just west of the bridge and has 18 tent sites and two pit toilets. Stoves are required and no fires are permitted.

The water from Tumbling Creek is often too silty to drink, but there is a creek just east of the campground with clear drinking water. This is the last water source for about 7.5km.

Tumbling Creek Campground to Helmet Falls Campground, 11.6km

From the Tumbling Creek Campground, the trail climbs steeply and relentlessly to the Wolverine Plateau. This is one of the most difficult climbs on the trail. The trail veers onto a slope overlooking the moraines of the Tumbling Glacier. Castle Mountain can be seen to the northeast. The trail climbs through old-growth larch forest and into the upper subalpine meadows of Wolverine Plateau. These meadows are a brilliant display of colour during the peak bloom in early August. A short side-trail on the right leads to the Wolverine Warden Station. Just over 3km from Tumbling Creek Campground, the trail reaches the Wolverine Pass junction. Head left for a short side-trip to the pass. Continue straight ahead for the Rockwall Pass. The Rockwall Pass is probably the scenic highpoint on the trail. The 4km precipice of the Rockwall between Mount Drysdale and Limestone Peak (2878m) dominates the view to the northeast. The trail continues through the beautiful alpine meadows of Rockwall Pass before descending to cross over a stream. After the stream, there is one more climb to the top of Limestone Summit at the end of Rockwall Pass. The trail passes through another flat meadow en route. From Limestone Summit, the trail descends to the Helmet Falls Campground. There is good view of Helmet Falls, with a total drop of 352m, along the way. Mount Goodsir (3562m) can be seen northeast from the falls. The Helmet Falls Campground has 18 tent sites and two pit toilets; a stove is required, as fires are not permitted.

Helmet Falls Campground to Paint Pots Trailhead, 15.5km

From the campground, the trail follows the Helmet Creek Trail, which
is mostly downhill and very slight in gradient, to its junction with the
Ochre Creek Trail. The trail gently descends through a lush subalpine
forest and crosses a suspension bridge over Helmet Creek. From the
bridge, there is a good view to the west of the Rockwall, Helmet
Mountain and part of the Wasmawapta Icefield. The trail climbs
through forest and then descends to Ochre Creek. The trail crosses
the creek to the campground at the Helmet/Ochre Creek Junction.
There are six tent sites, a pit toilet and firewood. The junction is just
beyond the campground. Turn right and follow all signs to Highway
93. The trail reaches the ochre beds at Paint Pots (see Trail 43 for the
cultural history of the area) and then crosses the Vermillion River on
a suspension bridge before reaching the Paint Pots trailhead and
parking area. The Paint Pots trailhead is 12.9km north of the Floe Lake
trailhead on Highway 93.

TRAIL 41: KAUFMANN LAKE TRAIL

Distance:	**15.1km one way**
Time:	**5hrs one way**
Rating:	**moderate**
Elevation change:	**570m**
Map:	**NTS 82N/1, 82N/8**
Base:	**Radium Hot Springs or Lake Louise**
Best time:	**July–September**

Kaufmann Lake was named for Peter Kaufmann, the father of Christian
and Hans Kaufman, two Swiss mountaineering guides who worked in
the Rockies between 1900 and 1906 leading many first ascents to
nearby peaks. Peter Kaufmann also guided in the area for a brief spell
in 1903. Kaufmann Lake is the most remote lake in Kootenay National
Park and an ideal location for a couple of days of solitude. Moose, elk,
and mule deer are often seen, along with the occasional grizzly bear.

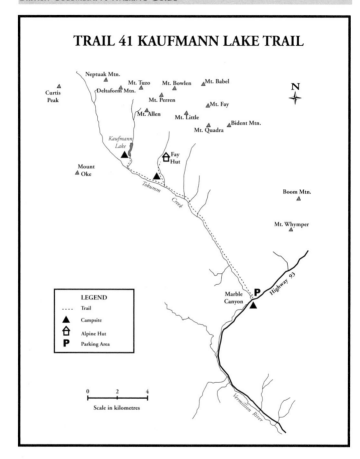

TRAIL 41 KAUFMANN LAKE TRAIL

Access

The trail begins at the Marble Canyon trailhead located on the north side of Highway 93, 17.2km west of the Castle Junction.

Trail Description

From the Marble Canyon trailhead, first follow the interpretive trail and turn right onto the Tokumm Creek Trail. Tokumm is a Stoney word for the area that is now known as Kootenay National Park. After the first 200m, the Tokumm Creek Trail joins an old mining cart-track. The short side-trail on the left leads to the upper waterfall in Marble Canyon. The main trail continues north through old-growth forest of Engelmann spruce and subalpine fir and crosses many small streams via bridges. At 3km, the trail narrows and drops down to edge of Tokumm Creek. From here, there are great views of the avalanche paths across the valley. For the next 7km, the trail more or less follows the creek. The trail passes a massive limestone boulder and crosses the large meltwater stream that originates from the Wenchemna Icefield. At 11.2km, the trail reaches the Fay Hut Junction. The trail to the right leads 2.4km up steep terrain to Fay Hut. Fay Hut was the first climbing hut built by the Alpine Club of Canada and dates back to 1927. The trail to Kaufmann Lake continues north, providing good views of Mount Oke (2920m). The trail soon reaches Tokumm Creek Campground. It is not unusual to see large chunks of consolidated avalanched snow along the creek even in summer. Small-scale mining for lead and zinc took place in this valley between 1914 and 1943. The valley is also prime bear habitat, and since the campsite is poorly located near avalanche slopes, campers might have a more peaceful rest further on at the Kaufmann Lake Campground. The trail continues on 2km to Kaufmann Lake, climbing up and down the gravel creek bed. After crossing the braided outflow of Kaufmann Lake, a directional sign points the way for the final climb, which is 243m in 1.5km. The trail first leads south towards the stream, climbing and descending, and then ascends steeply before smoothing out in a wet meadow. From here there is a view of Kaufmann Lake and views of Mount Allen (3301m), Mount Tuzo (3245m) to the east and Deltaform Mountain (3424m) to the west. The Kaufmann Lake Campground has six tent sites and a pit toilet. A stove is necessary, as fires are not permitted. Kaufmann Lake was once popular for sport fishing, but over the last century stocks have been seriously depleted.

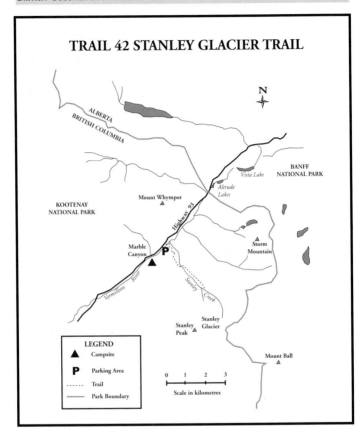

TRAIL 42 STANLEY GLACIER TRAIL

TRAIL 42: STANLEY GLACIER TRAIL

Distance:	**4.8km one way**
Time:	**2hrs one way**
Rating:	**moderate**
Elevation change:	**365m**

The Stanley Glacier

Map:	**NTS 82N/1**
Base:	**Radium Hot Springs or Lake Louise**
Best time:	**July–September**

Access

The trailhead and parking area are located 2.5km north of Marble Canyon on Highway 93.

Trail Description

This is a well-built trail that climbs through the 1968 Vermilion Pass burn area and ends at a great viewpoint 1.6km from Stanley Glacier. The first couple of kilometres are the steepest, as the trail climbs up the side of a moraine to the valley floor. A fire in 1968 burned old-growth forest, opening the ground up to sunlight and flowers. Many of the burnt trees are still standing. Stanley Glacier is at the head of a glacial valley that has been eroded into a classic U-shape. From the spectacular viewpoint at the end, Stanley Glacier is to the southwest; waterfalls caused by glacial meltwater are to the west; the sheer cliff face of the Guardwall is to the northwest; Mount Whymper lies to the north; and the avalanche slopes of Mount Ball are to the east.

TRAIL 43: PAINT POTS

Distance:	**2km return**
Time:	**45mins return**
Rating:	**easy**
Elevation change:	**minimal**
Map:	**NTS 82N/1**
Base:	**Radium Hot Springs or Lake Louise**
Best time:	**May–October**

Access
From Radium Hot Springs, follow Highway 93 north through the park 85km to the Paint Pots trailhead parking area.

Trail Description
This is a very short trail that marks the end or beginning of the Rockwall Trail, but is easily accessible to anyone short on time, and its cultural significance makes it well worth the stop.

The trail leads from the parking area through forest before crossing a bridge over Vermilion River and then leading to the ochre beds. The Paint Pots are a place of great spiritual significance, 'The place where the red clay spirit is taken'. An active cold spring that contains a great amount of dissolved iron bubbles to the surface forming muddy beds of red ochre. (Ochre is clay that is stained red or yellow with iron oxides – the colour depends on the amount of water and impurities.) Some of the exit holes for the springs have been formed into 'pots' by the accumulation of iron oxide around the rim. When the rim gets high enough, the weight of the contained water forces the water to follow another, less resistant, route and it forms another exit hole nearby. The old 'pot' dries up and forms a 'choked cone'. Some of the pots are active and others are just collected spring water and surface

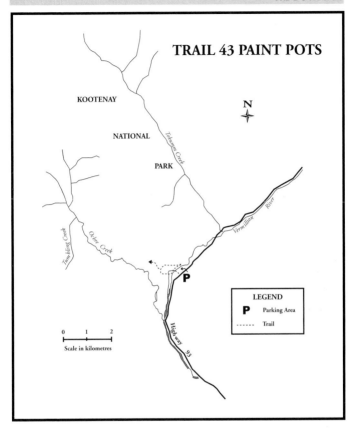

TRAIL 43 PAINT POTS

KOOTENAY

NATIONAL

PARK

N

Tokumm Creek

Vermillion River

Tumbling Creek

Ochre Creek

P

LEGEND

P   Parking Area

-----   Trail

Highway 93

0   1   2

Scale in kilometres

run-off. The ochre was used by the by the Kutenai people and was also a valuable trading commodity. The ochre was used to decorate tipis, clothing, shields and bodies, and to create rock paintings. The ochre was mixed with water and kneaded and shaped into flat cakes, which were baked in fire. The hardened cakes were then ground into a powder and mixed with fish oil or animal grease to be used as paint.

Near the ochre beds, notice the evidence of mining. At the beginning of the 20th century, the ochre was dug and sacked by hand and then hauled by horse-drawn wagons to the railway line, which is located 15 miles away at Mount Eisenhower. It was shipped by train to Calgary to be used as a pigment for paint. During the later years of ochre-mining in the 1920s, more sophisticated extraction methods were implemented; railcars, horse-drawn scoops, clay tiles and grinding machines were used to collect, roast and grind the iron oxide.

YOHO NATIONAL PARK

Background

'Yoho' is a Cree expression of awe and wonder, and beautifully sums up this area of snow-peaked mountains, incredible waterfalls and turquoise glacial lakes and streams. Yoho National Park was established in 1886 and includes 1310km^2 of the eastern Main Ranges of the Rocky Mountains. The park contains 28 peaks over 3000m in height; Canada's highest waterfall, Takakkaw Falls; and forested hills and valleys of cedar, hemlock, devil's club, spruce, pine, alpine fir, larch and rare orchids. The Ktunaxa and Shuswap were the first to use the area, crossing it to trade with the plains people. More recently, in 1858, James Hector explored the area as part of the Palliser Expedition.

In 1881, the Canadian Pacific Railway chose Yoho as the route to connect east and west, and Kicking Horse Pass was selected as the route across the Great Divide. The history of the park in these early years is closely linked to the railway. In 1886, the first train crossed. The very steep grade of 'the Big Hill' caused the railway a lot of problems, and the company was forced to construct safety switches. These were manned 24 hours a day to divert trains onto a runaway track. At every platform, they had to check the brakes. In 1909, the Spiral Tunnels were complete, essentially 9km of track that looped out from the main direction of the line to pass through the two mountains. The Canadian Pacific Railway started the tourism trade in Yoho by building lodges and trails and hiring Swiss guides to lead treks. In 1927, a car road was built through the park giving access to everyone.

Yoho is part of the Rocky Mountain UNESCO World Heritage Site, and in 1989 Kicking Horse River was dedicated as a Canadian heritage river, significant as a classic example of a glacially fed moun-

Natural Bridge – Yoho National Park

Emerald Lake, Yoho National Park

tain river. James Hector's men named the river, which was called 'Wapta' by the First Nations people, Kicking Horse in 1858. The story is that a pack horse fell into the river and, while the men fought to save it, the other horses wandered off. As Hector retrieved his own horse, he was kicked in the chest and knocked unconscious.

Burgess Shale

The Burgess Shale is a UNESCO world heritage site and is one of the most significant fossil sites in the world, containing the finest Cambrian-age fossils ever found. The Burgess Shale Site on Fossil Ridge and the Mount Stephen Fossil Beds above the town of Field are both closed to the public except via guided tours. For information and schedules on guided hikes, contact: The Yoho-Burgess Shale Foundation, PO Box 148, Field, BC, V0A 1G0, email: burgshal@ rockies.net.

The beginning of Cambrian Age was marked by the explosion of multi-cellular life. Approximately 530 million years ago, fossilized marine organisms were buried in mud. Somehow, they survived both the pressure of kilometres of sediment that accumulated over time on top of them and the upheaval of mountain building. They were finally uncovered by erosion. Slabs came lose from this exposed bed of shale and slid down the steep slope to be discovered in 1909 by Charles Walcott, the world expert on Cambrian rocks and fossils and Secretary of the Smithsonian Institution. He split the slab of shale open to uncover the finest fossil impressions he had ever seen. Over five field seasons, he removed 65,000 fossils from Fossil Ridge and sent them to the Smithsonian, where they still remain.

The Burgess Shale findings were significant because in most fossils only hard parts like bones and shells are preserved, as either scavengers eat the soft body parts or they decompose. But the Burgess Shale fossils preserved soft body parts as well, delicate tissues, digestive tracts and muscle fibres, all of which contribute greatly to our present knowledge of Cambrian ecosystems. The Mount Stephen Fossil Beds, which can be seen from Field, are about the same age as the Burgess Shale. They were discovered by railway workers in 1886 who reported finding 'stone bugs'. This area is known for its abundant trilobites.

Lake O'Hara

The Lake O'Hara area has 25 lakes and ponds within a 5km radius, and represents the transition between high subalpine and alpine. The meadows here are so fragile that the park has put a quota system in place to limit the number of people who use the bus service to the lake. Some parts are subject to seasonal closures to protect grizzly bear habitat and to reduce the likelihood of human–bear encounters. Any number of people may hike the 13km in to the lake, but reservations are required for both the bus service and the backcountry campground. Reservations can be made up to three months in advance by phoning (250) 343-6433 or in person at the Field Visitor Centre.

Campgrounds

Campsites are available on a first-come, first-served basis only.

Kicking Horse Campground

Located 4km east of Field off the TransCanada Highway on the Yoho Valley Road
86 sites
Open May–October
Facilities: flush toilets, coin-operated showers, fire pits, firewood and well water

Takakkaw Falls Campground

Located at the end of the Yoho Valley Road
35 tent pads
Open end of June – mid-September
Facilities: toilets, fire pits, firewood, bear-proof food and rubbish storage, enclosed kitchen shelter and well water

Monarch Campground

Located 3km east of Field near the beginning of the Yoho Valley Road
38 sites plus eight tent sites for cyclists
Open end of June–September
Facilities: toilets, kitchen shelter and well water

Hoodoo Creek Campground

Located 23km west of Field, off the Trans-Canada Highway

106 sites
Open end of June to September
Facilities: flush toilets, running water, fire pits, firewood and kitchen shelters

Chancellor Peak Campground
Located 24km west of Field off the Trans-Canada Highway
56 sites
Open mid-May – mid-September
Facilities: pit toilets, kitchen shelters, fire pits and well water

TRAIL 44: ICELINE TRAIL

Distance:	**19.8km loop via Little Yoho Valley**
Time:	**full day or overnight**
Rating:	**moderate–difficult**
Elevation change:	**695m**
Map:	**NTS 82N/7, 82N/8, 82N/10**
Base:	**Field or Lake Louise**
Best time:	**Mid-July–September**

Access
From Field, follow Highway 1 east for 3.7km to the Yoho Valley Road. From Lake Louise, drive 22.3km west on Highway 1. Turn north and follow the steep road for 13km to the Whiskey Jack Hostel. The trailhead is the hostel parking area. Note that the Yoho Valley Road is only open in summer, mid-June to mid-October, depending on snow.

Trail Description
This trail roughly follows the route taken by Edward Whymper in 1901, following the edge of the Emerald Glacier to the Little Yoho Valley. The trail was built in 1987: it begins at the Whiskey Jack Hostel and climbs through a large avalanche path onto a bench, with great views of the Emerald Glacier above and Takakkaw Falls and the Daly Glacier across the valley. The avalanche slopes in Yoho are summer habitat for moose and elk – be on the lookout! The Yoho Valley area

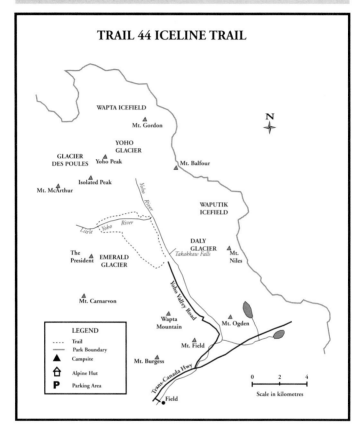

TRAIL 44 ICELINE TRAIL

is also the only large subalpine area in the park that hasn't succumbed to recent fires, and some of the spruce and fir trees are more than 500 years old. The route climbs through forests of spruce, fir and alder to the moraines, striated rock and icy pools of the Emerald Glacier. There is often snow in this area until mid-July. From here, follow all the signs to descend to the Little Yoho Valley. For a shorter route (17km loop), descend to the Little Yoho Valley via the Celeste Lake Trail. There is a campground and a cabin operated by the Alpine

Club of Canada in Little Yoho Valley. From the campground, the trail heads east to the Laughing Falls junction. From here, it is only 3.8km south on the Yoho Valley Trail to Takakkaw Falls.

TRAIL 45: EMERALD LAKE CIRCUIT

Distance:	**5.2km**
Time:	**1hr 30mins**
Rating:	**easy**

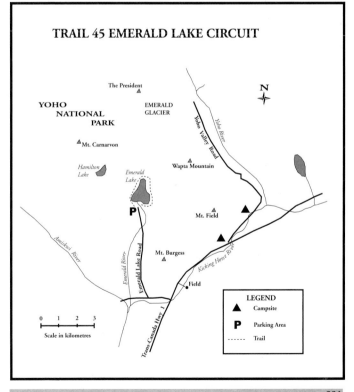

TRAIL 45 EMERALD LAKE CIRCUIT

The President ▲

YOHO
NATIONAL
PARK

EMERALD
GLACIER

▲ Mt. Carnarvon

Hamilton
Lake

Emerald
Lake

Yoho Valley Road

Yoho River

▲ Wapta Mountain

P

Mt. Field ▲

▲

Amiskwi River

Emerald River

Emerald Lake Road

Mt. Burgess
▲

▲

Kicking Horse River

• Field

N

	LEGEND	
▲		Campsite
P		Parking Area
.....		Trail

0 1 2 3
Scale in kilometres

Trans-Canada Hwy 1

Elevation change:	minimal
Map:	NTS 82N/7
Base:	Field or Lake Louise
Best time:	May–October

Access
From Field, drive west on Highway 1 and turn right onto the Emerald Lake Road. From Field, it is 11km to the parking area and trailhead at the end of the Emerald Lake Road.

Trail Description
Emerald Lake is known as one of the jewels of the Rockies and has been captured by many a photographer. Its spectacular colour is the result of finely ground rock flour suspended in the water, which occurs because the lake is fed with the meltwater of a glacier and not snow. Rock flour is as fine as dust, and its tiny particles reflect blue and green wavelengths of the light spectrum. A short trail around the lake provides views of the snow-capped mountains, the stunning glacier that feeds the lake and many species of birds. On the west side of the lake, especially in June and July, look out for rare wild orchids. On the east side, the vegetation changes to cedar-hemlock forests.

Alternative
Rent a canoe from Emerald Sports and Gift Store at Emerald Lake (tel: (250) 343-6000) and experience the spectacular scenery from a different perspective.

TRAIL 46: YOHO GLACIER MORAINE

Distance:	20.1km loop
Time:	full day or overnight
Rating:	moderate–difficult
Elevation change:	250m
Map:	NTS 82N/7, 82N/8, 82N/10
Base:	Field or Lake Louise
Best time:	July–September

Access

From Field, follow Highway 1 east for 3.7km to the Yoho Valley Road. From Lake Louise, drive 22.3km west on Highway 1. Follow the steep Yoho Valley Road to its end, just over 13km, at the Takakkaw Falls parking area. Note that the Yoho Valley Road is only open in summer, mid-June to mid-October, depending on snow.

Trail Description

Ask staff at the Field Visitor Centre if the bridge is in before beginning this trail.

Many variations of this trail exist, but this route follows the trail from Takakkaw Falls to Laughing Falls to Twin Falls and over the Whaleback Trail, returning to Takakkaw Falls. The trail begins near Takakkaw Falls. Takakkaw means 'magnificent' in Cree, and describes the 380m thundering plummet of water that originates from the Daly Glacier. It is technically Canada's highest waterfall, with a freefall drop of 254m (Della Falls is higher but has three drops). July is the peak melting time for glaciers and this is when Takakkaw Falls is at its most mighty.

From Takakkaw Falls, it is only a short hike to Laughing Falls. Laughing Falls cascades from the Little Yoho Valley, a hanging valley that is 500m above the main valley floor. At 3.7km the trail reaches a junction with a side-trail leading to Duchesnay Lake. The main trail shortly reaches the Laughing Falls Campground. Just beyond the campground, the trail crosses over Twin Falls Creek and follows the Yoho River for a while. Then the trail veers right to enter back into

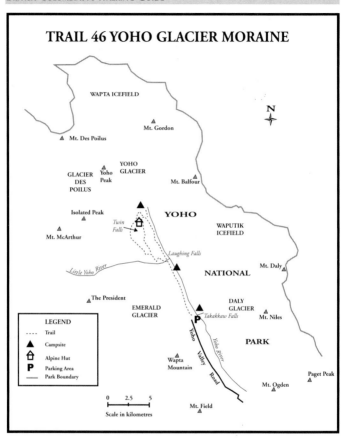

TRAIL 46 YOHO GLACIER MORAINE

WAPTA ICEFIELD

Mt. Gordon

Mt. Des Poilus

YOHO GLACIER

GLACIER DES POILUS

Yoho Peak

Mt. Balfour

Isolated Peak

YOHO

Twin Falls

WAPUTIK ICEFIELD

Mt. McArthur

Laughing Falls

Little Yoho River

Mt. Daly

NATIONAL

The President

EMERALD GLACIER

DALY GLACIER

Takakkaw Falls

Mt. Niles

PARK

Wapta Mountain

Yoho Valley Road

Yoho River

Paget Peak

Mt. Ogden

Mt. Field

LEGEND

- - - - Trail
▲ Campsite
⌂ Alpine Hut
P Parking Area
—— Park Boundary

0   2.5   5
Scale in kilometres

the valley of the Twin Falls Creek before reaching another junction. The trail to the right leads north 2.4km up to Yoho Glacier, which makes a great side-trip from the Twin Falls Campground. The left trail descends to the Twin Falls Campground. Just past the campground, the trail climbs up towards the Whaleback junction, and the roar of Twin Falls gets louder and louder. Twin Falls is twin cascades of water that plummet over a limestone cliff. The junction is just north of Twin

Looking east from Black Tusk (photo by Jonathan Deakin)

Trail up the Tusk (photo by Jonathan Deakin)

Falls Chalet (operated by the Alpine Club of Canada). Turn right onto the Whaleback Trail. The trail climbs steadily with great views of the Waputik Icefield and Mount Balfour, the highest peak in the area at 3272m. The trail heads south along the cliff edge. There is a bridge over Twin Falls Creek. Because this area is in an avalanche slide path, the bridge is dismantled every winter to avoid its destruction.

After the bridge, the next 1.5km are the highlight of the Yoho Valley, with spectacular views of the surrounding peaks and glaciers. The trail climbs up from the creek through the forest and emerges in subalpine meadows. Mount Balfour can be seen to the east, Yoho Peak to the northeast, and Mount Daly and Mount Niles to the south. Just before the south end of Whaleback Mountain, the trail veers right. A short trail straight ahead leads to a viewpoint overlooking the Yoho Valley. The main trail descends steeply via switchbacks down to the Little Yoho Valley. At the junction, the trail to the right leads to the Little Yoho Valley Campground. The Iceline Trail is straight ahead, and the trail to the left leads back to the Yoho Valley Trail and back to Takakkaw Falls.

TRAIL 47: YOHO PASS

Distance:	**12.1km one way**
Time:	**5hrs**
Rating:	**moderate**
Elevation change:	**530m**
Map:	**NTS 82N/7, 82N/8, 82N/10**
Base:	**Field or Lake Louise**
Best time:	**July–September**

Access

From Field, drive west on Highway 1 and turn right onto the Emerald Lake Road. From Field, it is 11km to the parking area and trailhead at the end of the Emerald Lake Road. Hikers wishing to hike only one way can shuttle their cars so that one is at the end at the Whiskey Jack Hostel near Takakkaw Falls and another is at the beginning. Another option is to camp at Takakkaw Falls and hike back the next day.

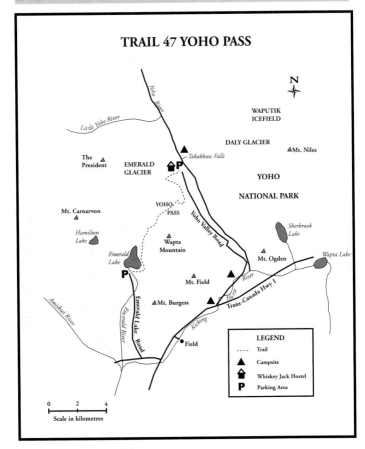

TRAIL 47 YOHO PASS

N

WAPUTIK
ICEFIELD

DALY GLACIER

▲Mt. Niles

Yoho River

Little Yoho River

The
President ▲

EMERALD
GLACIER

▲ *Takakkaw Falls*

YOHO

NATIONAL PARK

YOHO
PASS

Yoho Valley Road

Mt. Carnarvon
▲

*Hamilton
Lake*

Emerald
Lake

▲
Wapta
Mountain

Sherbrook
Lake

▲
Mt. Ogden

Wapta Lake

Amiskwi River

P

▲Mt. Field

Emerald River

Emerald Lake Road

▲Mt. Burgess

▲

Kicking *Horse River*

Trans-Canada Hwy 1

● Field

LEGEND

- - - - Trail

▲ Campsite

⌂ Whiskey Jack Hostel

P Parking Area

0   2   4
Scale in kilometres

Trail Description

First, follow the Emerald Lake Trail around the lake to the Yoho Pass junction (about 1.5km). The trail climbs gently through a valley. The trail passes through a gravel outwash plain and then climbs steadily and steeply to Yoho Pass. There is a good view back to Emerald Lake and the Van Horne Range. From the pass, the trail descends to Yoho

Convergence of Two Rivers, Yoho National Park

Lake. The lake is about 8km from the beginning. There is a campground at Yoho Lake with eight tent sites, pit toilet, a bear pole to hang food and a great view of Wapta Mountain. From the lake, the trail descends passing Hidden Lakes to the Whiskey Jack Hostel near Takakkaw Falls.

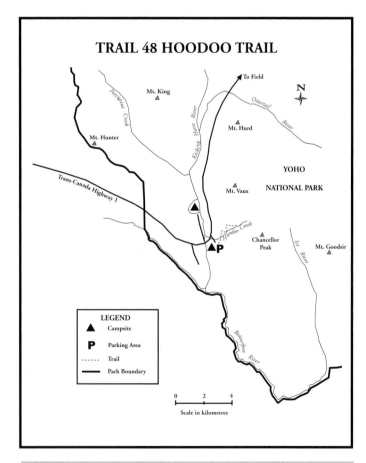

TRAIL 48 HOODOO TRAIL

To Field

N

Porcupine Creek

Mt. King

Kicking Horse River

Ottertail River

Mt. Hunter

Mt. Hurd

Trans-Canada Highway 1

YOHO

Mt. Vaux

NATIONAL PARK

Hoodoo Creek

▲P

Chancellor Peak

Ice River

Mt. Goodsir

LEGEND

▲ Campsite

P Parking Area

----- Trail

—— Park Boundary

Beaverfoot River

0   2   4
Scale in kilometres

TRAIL 48: HOODOO TRAIL

Distance:	**3.2km return**
Time:	**3–4hrs**
Rating:	**moderate**
Elevation change:	**455m**
Map:	**NTS 82N/2**
Base:	**Field or Lake Louise**
Best time:	**July–September**

Access
Follow Highway 1 west from Field 23km to the Hoodoo Creek Campground. The trailhead is at the creek between loops F and T in the campground.

Trail Description
This a short but steep, dry trail to the hoodoos. Make sure to bring water. The hoodoos are pillars of naturally cemented gravel, sand and silt – glacial debris. Many of the pillars have large stones that rest perilously on top of them. These rock caps act as rain hats, shielding the areas below from rain and erosion. Water erodes deep furrows around the capstones, shaping the pillar formations.

MOUNT ROBSON PROVINCIAL PARK

Background
The Texqakallt Nation, the area's earliest known inhabitants, called Mount Robson Yuh-hai-has-kun or 'The mountain of the spiral road' because of its layered appearance. It is the highest peak in the entire Canadian Rockies and stands at an awe-inspiring 3954m. The Texqakallt were Shuswap people of the Upper North Thompson River and were almost completely nomadic. They wore marmot skins and slept in the snow out in the open, warming their feet by the fire. They hunted bighorn sheep, mountain goats, moose and marmots, fished for salmon and trout, and ate berries. Mount Robson Provincial Park protects the

spectacular alpine areas, rivers, lakes and prime wetland habitat. From a conservation perspective, the most important feature of this park is the headwaters of the Fraser River, one of the world's greatest rivers. It is the same river that empties over 1200km away in Vancouver into the Pacific Ocean. The eastern section of the park is best known for the Ramparts, a chain of impressive rock formations created by glacial movement. The park contains four biogeoclimatic zones and 182 bird species, 42 mammal species, four amphibian and one reptile species.

Campgrounds
Campsite reservations can be made at Robson Meadows Campground or through Discover Camping by calling 1-800-689-9025 (after March 1st).

Robson Meadows Campground
Located across from Mount Robson Park Headquarters on Highway 16
125 sites
Facilities: flush toilets, showers, firewood, drinking water and rubbish bins.
Campsites may be reserved.

Robson River Campground
Located next to Mount Robson Park Headquarters on Highway 16
19 sites
Facilities: flush toilets, showers, firewood, drinking water and rubbish bins.

Lucerne Campground
Located 34km west of Jasper on Highway 16 on Yellowhead Lake
32 sites
Facilities: flush toilets, showers, firewood, drinking water and rubbish bins.

TRAIL 49: BERG LAKE TRAIL

Distance:	**21km one way**
Time:	**2–5 days**
Rating:	**moderate–difficult**
Elevation change:	**800m**
Map:	**NTS 83E/3**
Base:	**Valemount or Jasper**
Best time:	**June–September**

Hikers **must** register for the Berg Lake Trail at the Mount Robson Visitor Centre, which is open from May through September. The Mount Robson Park Headquarters and Visitor Centre is located at the western entrance to the park, 84km west from Jasper on Highway 16 or 18km east from Tete Jaune Cache.

Access
From the Mount Robson Visitor Centre, turn north onto the paved side-road and follow it 2km to its end at the Berg Lake trailhead parking area.

Trail Description
Trailhead to Whitehorn, 11km
The first part of the trail follows a wide path along the Robson River. There are boardwalks over the bog areas. Just before the Kinney Lake campsite at 7km there may be a meandering stream – it depends on the amount of run-off from the mountains. After Kinney Lake, the trail crosses over a few streams where there are bridges. The trail then reaches the junction with the horse trail. The main trail veers off to the right climbing upwards through the forest and then along the cliff edges of the river. There is a section of about 20 minutes where the trail goes up and down before descending down to the Robson River. The trail crosses over a couple of bridges and then reaches the flats. At the end of the flats, the trail ascends 100m up to the Whitehorn Campsite. Just before the campsite, the trail descends back down to

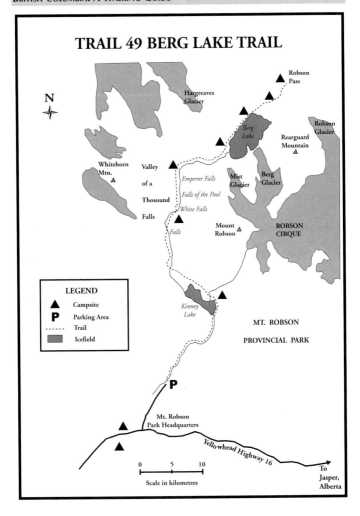

TRAIL 49 BERG LAKE TRAIL

N

Hargreaves
Glacier

Robson
Pass

Robson
Glacier

Berg
Lake

Rearguard
Mountain

Whitehorn
Mtn.

Valley

of a

Thousand

Falls

Emperor Falls

Falls of the Pool

White Falls

Falls

Mist
Glacier

Berg
Glacier

ROBSON
CIRQUE

Mount
Robson

Kinney
Lake

MT. ROBSON

PROVINCIAL PARK

LEGEND

▲ Campsite

P Parking Area

- - - Trail

▨ Icefield

P

Mt. Robson
Park Headquarters

Yellowhead Highway 16

To
Jasper,
Alberta

0   5   10

Scale in kilometres

the river at Whitehorn. Cross the suspension bridge to reach the tent sites or to continue on the trail.

Whitehorn to Emperor Falls, 5km
At the end of Whitehorn Campsite, the trail first follows the river and then crosses another suspension bridge. The trail then climbs up the hillside to a great view of White Falls. This is the steepest part of the trail. After about 30mins, the trail levels out and reaches the rest area at Falls of the Pool. The trail climbs steadily again before eventually levelling out once more. Emperor Falls can be seen in the distance. The trail descends a little to a junction. The trail to the right leads to Emperor Falls. The main trail goes to the left and climbs steeply to the Emperor Falls Campsite (about 15 minutes).

Emperor Falls to Berg Lake, 5km
This last part of the trail is the most beautiful and easy compared to the steep ascents of the previous sections. The trail follows the river and then enters the forest. It leaves the forest at an avalanche slide area with a spectacular view of Mist Glacier. The trail goes along the rocks and then descends down to the river. The trail then heads towards Mist Glacier and Berg Glacier, crossing a couple of creeks over log bridges. The Marmot Campsite is at the tip of Berg Lake. From here, it is only 2km further along the lake to the Berg Lake Campsite. Watch out for deer at the Berg Lake Campsite and look out for pieces of the Berg Glacier which sometimes calve off and fall into the lake.

TRAIL 50: MOUNT FITZWILLIAM TRAIL

Distance:	**13.5km one way**
Time:	**overnight**
Rating:	**difficult**
Elevation change:	**1000m**
Map:	**NTS 83D/15**
Base:	**Valemount or Jasper**
Best time:	**June–September**

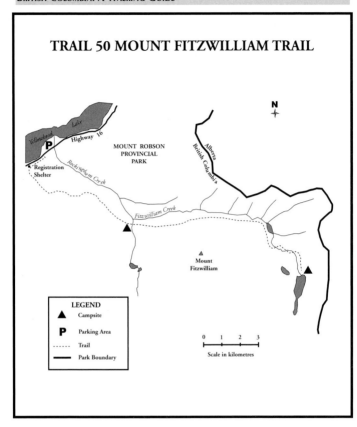

TRAIL 50 MOUNT FITZWILLIAM TRAIL

LEGEND

▲ Campsite

P Parking Area

- - - - - Trail

——— Park Boundary

0 1 2 3

Scale in kilometres

Access

The trailhead is 54km east of the Mount Robson Park Headquarters and Visitor Centre and 4km east of the Lucerne Campground on the shores of Yellowhead Lake. Yellowhead Lake, Yellowhead Mountain, Yellowhead Pass and the town of Tete Jaune Cache are all named after Pierre Bostonais, a Metis guide who came to the area with a group of Hudson Bay Company traders in 1820. In the early 1800s a village of Iroquois people travelled occasionally to Kamloops to trade their furs.

Bostonais was a dark-skinned, fair-haired Metis who was nicknamed in French 'Tete Jaune' or 'Yellow Head'.

Note: Mosquitoes can be a big problem on this trail during wet periods.

Trail Description

In 1863, Walter Butler Cheadle and William Wentworth Fitzwilliam, also known as Viscount Milton, were camping on the shores of Yellowhead Lake and decided to name the 'cone-like and terraced' mountain Fitzwilliam. At the trailhead and parking area, there are pit toilets and an information shelter. Make sure to register at the shelter prior to beginning the hike. To get to the main trail, cross over to the south side of the highway and walk 1.2km along the pipeline. From here, the trail switchbacks for the next 2km before levelling out. At 7.2km, the trail reaches Rockingham Creek Campsite with good views of Mount Fitzwilliam. The campsite has a pit toilet and a bear pole. Beyond the campsite, the trail becomes rough and not very well defined in some spots as it heads around the base of Mount Fitzwilliam. The trail leads through open meadows and passes along the edge of a rock slide. At 11km, the trail reaches a headwall. Carefully follow the markers up the left side of the gully, which can be very slippery. Some 2.5km further is a wilderness campsite at the end of an alpine lake.

APPENDIX A
VANCOUVER

Most visitors to British Columbia fly into Vancouver and spend a little or a lot of time there. Vancouver is a bustling, multi-cultural city with lots to do and see. It's easy to get around by foot, bicycle, car, bus or the skytrain. Make sure to visit Chinatown, the Museum of Anthropology at the University of British Columbia, Granville Island, Stanley Park and Gastown. Vancouver has cafes on every corner, micro-breweries, beaches, a fantastic nightlife, great shopping and friendly, laid-back people.

Tourism Information

Vancouver Tourist Info Centre (Tourism Vancouver)

200 Burrard Street

Vancouver, BC

V6C 3L

Tel. (604) 683-2000

www.tourismvancouver.com

Accommodation

Hostelling International Vancouver – Downtown

1114 Burnaby Street

Vancouver, BC

V6E 1P1

Tel. (604) 684-4565

Tel. 1-888-203-4302

Email: van-downtown@hihostels.bc.ca

Hostelling International Vancouver – Jericho Beach

1515 Discovery Street

Vancouver, BC
V6R 4K5
Tel. (604) 224-3208
Tel. 1-888-203-4303
Email: van-jericho@hihostels.bc.ca

Resources

Vancouver Sun Newspaper – www.vancouversun.com

The Georgia Straight – Vancouver's free weekly arts and entertainment newspaper – wwwstraight.com

APPENDIX B
NORTHWEST COAST NATIVE CULTURES

British Columbia's First Nations people have lived in this area for thousands of years. Archaeological evidence indicates that ancestors of today's First Nations people have occupied this area since the end of the last ice age, 10,000–12,000 years ago. Today, BC has 17.5% of Canada's Aboriginal people, with a population of about 140,000. They make up 3.8% of BC's population. BC has 197 different First Nations bands and 33 tribal councils.

The following are just a few starting points to learn more about Northwest Coast Native Cultures.

Resources

British Columbia First Nations – www.bcfn.org

This is a directory of First Nations Tribal Councils, associations and organizations, and aboriginal businesses in BC.

Aboriginal Tourism Association of British Columbia
www.atbc.bc.ca

Raven's Eye
BC and Yukon's aboriginal news publication
www.ammsa.com/raven/index.htm

Books

As Far As I Know: Reminiscences of an Ahousaht Elder, by Peter Webster, Campbell River Museum and Archives, 1983

Chiefs of Sea and Sky, by George F. MacDonald, Vancouver: UBC Press, 1989

During My Time: Florence Edenshaw Davidson, A Haida Woman, by Margaret Blackman, Vancouver: Douglas and McIntyre, 1982

Eagle Transforming: the Art of Robert Davidson, by Robert Davidson, University of Washington Press, 1994

'Kutenai Tales', by Franz Boas, Smithsonian Institution, *Bureau of American Ethnology Bulletin* 59, 1918

My Heart Soars, by Chief Dan George, Saanichton: Hancock House, 1974

My Spirit Soars, by Chief Dan George, Vancouver: Hancock House, 1982

Our Tellings: Interior Salish Stories of the Nlak7kapmx People, compiled and edited by Darwin Hanna Mamie Henry, Vancouver: UBC Press, 1996

They Write Their Dreams on the Rock Forever: Rock Writings in the Stein River Valley of BC, by Annie York, Richard Daly, Chris Arnett, Vancouver: Talon Books, 1993

Those Born at Koona: The Totem Poles of the Haida Village Skedans Queen Charlotte Islands, by John and Carolyn Smyly, Vancouver: Hancock House Publishers, 1981

APPENDIX C
USEFUL ADDRESSES

Tourism Information
Tourism BC
Parliament Buildings
Victoria, BC
V8V 1X4
Tel. 1-800-HELLO-BC (within North America)
www.hellobc.com

National and Provincial Parks
Parks Canada Information – British Columbia
Box 129
23433 Mavis Avenue
Fort Langley, BC
V1M 2R5
Tel. (604) 666-1280
Email: Parks_Infobc@pch.gc.ca
http://parkscanada.pch.gc.ca

BC Parks Headquarters
PO Box 9398 Stn Prov Govt
Victoria, BC
V8W 9M9
Tel. (250) 387-5002
Email: parkinfo@victoria1.gov.bc.ca
www.env.gov.bc.ca/bcparks/

Vancouver Island
Juan de Fuca Provincial Park
BC Parks

South Vancouver Island District
2930 Trans Canada Highway
Victoria, BC
V9E 1K3
Tel. (250) 391-2300
Fax (250) 478-9211
www.bcparks.gov.bc.ca

Pacific Rim National Park Reserve
Box 280
Ucluelet, BC
V0R 3A0
Tel. (250) 726-7721
Fax (250) 726-4720
Email: pacrim_info@pch.gc.ca
West Coast Trail Reservations: Canada/USA: Tel. 1-800-HELLO-BC
Overseas: Tel. (250) 387-1642

Strathcona Provincial Park and Flores Island Provincial Park
BC Parks
District Manager
Rathtrevor Beach Provincial Park
Box 1479
Parksville, BC
V9P 2H4
Tel. (250) 954-4600
Fax (250) 248-8584

Cape Scott Provincial Park
BC Parks
1812 Miracle Beach Drive
Black Creek, BC
V0R 1C0
Tel. (250) 337-2400
Fax (250) 337-5695

Haida Gwaii

Naikoon Provincial Park

BC Parks

Area Supervisor

Box 19

Tlell, BC

V0T 1Y0

Tel. (250) 557-4390

Fax (250) 557-4390

Gwaii Haanas National Park Reserve/Haida Heritage Site

PO Box 37

Queen Charlotte, BC

V0T 1S0

Tel. (250) 559-8818

Fax (250) 559-3866

Whistler/Squamish

BC Parks

District Manager

Alice Lake Provincial Park

Box 220

Brackendale, BC

V0N 1H0

Tel. (604) 898-3678

Fax (604) 898-4171

Hope/Manning

Manning Provincial Park

BC Parks

Manning Provincial Park

Box 3, Manning Park, BC

V0X 1R0

Tel. (250) 840-8836

Fax (250) 840-8700

Stein Valley
Stein Valley Nlaka'pamux Heritage Park
BC Parks
1210 McGill Road
Kamloops, BC
V2C 6N6
Tel. (250) 851-3000

Mount Revelstoke/Glacier
Glacier National Park/ Mount Revelstoke National Park
PO Box 350
Revelstoke, BC
V0E 2S0
Tel. (250) 837-7500
Fax (250) 837-7536
Email: revglacier_reception@pch.gc.ca

The Kootenays
Kokanee Glacier Provincial Park
BC Parks
West Kootenay District
Site 8, Comp. 5, R.R. #3
Nelson, BC
V1L 5P6
Tel. (250) 422-4200
Fax (250) 422-3326

Purcell Wilderness Conservancy
BC Parks
Area Supervisor
Kootenay District
Box 118
Wasa, BC
V0B 2K0

Tel. (250) 422-4206
Fax (250) 422-3326

BC Rockies
Kootenay National Park
PO Box 220
Radium Hot Springs, BC
V0A 1M0
Tel. (250) 347-9615
Fax (250) 347-9980
Email: kootenay_reception@pch.gc.ca

Yoho National Park
PO Box 99
Field, BC
V0A 1G0
Tel. (250) 343-6783
Fax (250) 343-6012
Email: yoho_info@pch.gc.ca

Mount Robson Provincial Park
BC Parks
Mount Robson Area Office
Box 579
Valemount, BC
V0E 1Z0
Tel. (250) 566-4325
Fax (250) 566-9777

APPENDIX D:
TRAIL TABLE

Trail	Region	Trail	Distance	Rating	Park/Location
1	Vancouver Island	Juan de Fuca Marine Trail	47km	Mod/Difficult	Juan de Fuca Provincial Park
2	Vancouver Island	East Sooke Coast Trail	10km	Mod/Difficult	East Sooke Regional Park
3	Vancouver Island	Della Falls Trail	16km	Moderate	Strathcona Provincial Park
4	Vancouver Island	West Coast Trail	75km	Difficult	Pacific Rim National Park
5	Vancouver Island	Wickannish Trail	5km	Easy	Pacific Rim National Park
6	Vancouver Island	Schooner Trail	2.08km	Easy	Pacific Rim National Park
7	Vancouver Island	Willowbrae Trail	2.8km	Easy	Pacific Rim National Park
8	Vancouver Island	The Ahousaht Wild Side Trail	16km	Moderate	Flores Island Provincial Park
9	Vancouver Island	Cape Scott Trail	23.6km	Mod/-Difficult	Cape Scott Provincial Park
10	Haida Gwaii	Spirit Lake Trail	3km	Easy-Moderate	Skidegate
11	Haida Gwaii	Sleeping Beauty	3km	Difficult	Queen Charlotte City
12	Haida Gwaii	RileyCreek/Rennell Sound	2.5km	Easy-Moderate	Rennell Sound
13	Haida Gwaii	Pesuta Trail	10km	Easy	Naikoon Provincial Park
14	Haida Gwaii	East Beach Hike	89km	Moderate	Naikoon Provincial Park
15	Haida Gwaii	Tow Hill/Blow Hole		Moderate	Naikoon Provincial Park
16	Haida Gwaii	Cape Fife Trail		Moderate	Naikoon Provincial Park

Trail	Region	Trail	Distance	Rating	Park/Location
17	Squamish/Whistler	Stawamus Chief	6km	Mod/Difficult	Squamish
18	Squamish/Whistler	Black Tusk/Garibaldi Lake	9km	Moderate	Whistler
19	Squamish/Whistler	Brandywine Falls	1km	Easy	Whistler
20	Squamish/Whistler	Shadow Lake	3km	Easy	Whistler
21	Squamish/Whistler	Nairn Falls	3km	Easy	Whistler
22	Manning Park	Heather Trail	20km	Moderate	Manning Provincial Park
23	Manning Park	Skyline 1 Trail	20.4km	Difficult	Manning Provincial Park
24	Manning Park	Pacific Crest/Castle Creek	24km	Mod/Difficult	Manning Provincial Park
25	Manning Park	Lightning Lake Loop	9km	Easy	Manning Provincial Park
26	Stein Valley	Lower Stein Valley	28km	Moderate	Stein Valley Nlaka'pamux Heritage
27	Revelstoke/Glacier	Summit Trail	10km	Moderate	Mount Revelstoke National Park
28	Revelstoke/Glacier	Eva Lake Trail	6km	Easy	Mount Revelstoke National Park
29	Revelstoke/Glacier	Jade Lakes Trail	9km	Moderate	Mount Revelstoke National Park
30	Revelstoke/Glacier	Giant Cedars Trail	0.5km	Easy	Mount Revelstoke National Park
31	Revelstoke/Glacier	Asulkan Valley Trail	6.5km	Mod/Difficult	Glacier National Park
32	Revelstoke/Glacier	Glacier Crest Trail	4.8km	Mod/Difficult	Glacier National Park
33	Revelstoke/Glacier	Avalanche Crest Trail	4.2km	Mod/Difficult	Glacier National Park
34	Revelstoke/Glacier	Abbott Ridge	5.0km	Mod/Difficult	Glacier National Park
35	Revelstoke/Glacier	Hermit Trail	2.8km	Difficult	Glacier National Park

Trail	Region	Trail	Distance	Rating	Park/Location
36	The Kootenays	Pulpit Rock Hike	1km	Moderate	Nelson
37	The Kootenays	Gibson Lake	9km	Moderate	Kokanee Glacier Provincial Park
38	The Kootenays	Earl Grey Pass Trail	61km	Difficult	Purcell Wilderness Conservancy
39	The Kootenays	Lake of the Hanging Glacier	8km	Moderate	Lake of The Hanging Glacier
40	BC Rockies	Rockwall Trail	55km	Mod/Difficult	Kootenay National Park
41	BC Rockies	Kaufmann Lake Trail	15.1km	Moderate	Kootenay National Park
42	BC Rockies	Stanley Glacier Trail	4.8km	Moderate	Kootenay National Park
43	BC Rockies	Paint Pots	2km	Easy	Kootenay National Park
44	BC Rockies	Iceline Trail	19.8km	Mod/Difficult	Yoho National Park
45	BC Rockies	Emerald Lake Circuit	5.2km	Easy	Yoho National Park
46	BC Rockies	Yoho Glacier Moraine	20.1km	Mod/Difficult	Yoho National Park
47	BC Rockies	Yoho pass	12.1km	Moderate	Yoho National Park
48	BC Rockies	Hoodoo Trail	3.2km	Moderate	Yoho National Park
49	BC Rockies	Berg Lake Trail	23kmy	Mod/Difficult	Mount Robson Provincial Park
50	BC Rockies	Mount Fitzwilliam Trail	13.5km/	Difficult	Mount Robson Provincial Park

LISTING OF CICERONE GUIDES

LISTING OF CICERONE GUIDES

CENTRAL HIGHLANDS
  6 LONG DISTANCE WALKS
WALKING THE GALLOWAY HILLS
WALKING IN THE HEBRIDES
NORTH TO THE CAPE
THE ISLAND OF RHUM
THE ISLE OF SKYE A Walker's Guide
WALKS IN THE LAMMERMUIRS
WALKING IN THE LOWTHER HILLS
THE SCOTTISH GLENS SERIES
  1 - CAIRNGORM GLENS
  2 - ATHOLL GLENS
  3 - GLENS OF RANNOCH
  4 - GLENS OF TROSSACH
  5 - GLENS OF ARGYLL
  6 - THE GREAT GLEN
  7 - THE ANGUS GLENS
  8 - KNOYDART TO MORVERN
  9 - THE GLENS OF ROSS-SHIRE
SCOTTISH RAILWAY WALKS
SCRAMBLES IN LOCHABER
SCRAMBLES IN SKYE
SKI TOURING IN SCOTLAND
THE SPEYSIDE WAY
TORRIDON - A Walker's Guide
WALKS FROM THE WEST HIGHLAND
  RAILWAY
THE WEST HIGHLAND WAY
WINTER CLIMBS NEVIS & GLENCOE

IRELAND
IRISH COASTAL WALKS
THE IRISH COAST TO COAST
THE MOUNTAINS OF IRELAND

WALKING AND TREKKING IN THE ALPS
WALKING IN THE ALPS
100 HUT WALKS IN THE ALPS
CHAMONIX to ZERMATT
GRAND TOUR OF MONTE ROSA
  Vol. 1 and Vol. 2
TOUR OF MONT BLANC

FRANCE, BELGIUM AND LUXEMBOURG
WALKING IN THE ARDENNES
ROCK CLIMBS BELGIUM & LUX.
THE BRITTANY COASTAL PATH
CHAMONIX - MONT BLANC
  Walking Guide
WALKING IN THE CEVENNES
CORSICAN HIGH LEVEL ROUTE: GR20
THE ECRINS NATIONAL PARK
WALKING THE FRENCH ALPS: GR5
WALKING THE FRENCH GORGES
FRENCH ROCK
WALKING IN THE HAUTE SAVOIE
WALKING IN THE LANGUEDOC
TOUR OF THE OISANS: GR54
WALKING IN PROVENCE
THE PYRENEAN TRAIL: GR10
THE TOUR OF THE QUEYRAS
ROBERT LOUIS STEVENSON TRAIL

WALKING IN TARENTAISE &
  BEAUFORTAIN ALPS
ROCK CLIMBS IN THE VERDON
TOUR OF THE VANOISE
WALKS IN VOLCANO COUNTRY

FRANCE/SPAIN
ROCK CLIMBS IN THE PYRENEES
WALKS & CLIMBS IN THE PYRENEES
THE WAY OF ST JAMES
  Le Puy to Santiago - Walker's
THE WAY OF ST JAMES
  Le Puy to Santiago - Cyclist's

SPAIN AND PORTUGAL
WALKING IN THE ALGARVE
ANDALUSIAN ROCK CLIMBS
BIRDWATCHING IN MALLORCA
COSTA BLANCA ROCK
COSTA BLANCA WALKS VOL 1
COSTA BLANCA WALKS VOL 2
WALKING IN MALLORCA
ROCK CLIMBS IN MAJORCA, IBIZA &
  TENERIFE
WALKING IN MADEIRA
THE MOUNTAINS OF CENTRAL SPAIN
THE SPANISH PYRENEES GR11 2nd Ed.
WALKING IN THE SIERRA NEVADA
WALKS & CLIMBS IN THE PICOS DE
  EUROPA
VIA DE LA PLATA

SWITZERLAND
ALPINE PASS ROUTE, SWITZERLAND
THE BERNESE ALPS A Walking Guide
CENTRAL SWITZERLAND
THE JURA: HIGH ROUTE & SKI
  TRAVERSES
WALKING IN TICINO, SWITZERLAND
THE VALAIS, SWITZERLAND.
  A Walking Guide

GERMANY, AUSTRIA AND EASTERN EUROPE
MOUNTAIN WALKING IN AUSTRIA
WALKING IN THE BAVARIAN ALPS
WALKING IN THE BLACK FOREST
THE DANUBE CYCLE WAY
GERMANY'S ROMANTIC ROAD
WALKING IN THE HARZ MOUNTAINS
KING LUDWIG WAY
KLETTERSTEIG Northern Limestone Alps
WALKING THE RIVER RHINE TRAIL
THE MOUNTAINS OF ROMANIA
WALKING IN THE SALZKAMMERGUT
HUT-TO-HUT IN THE STUBAI ALPS
THE HIGH TATRAS

SCANDANAVIA
WALKING IN NORWAY
ST OLAV'S WAY

ITALY AND SLOVENIA
ALTA VIA - HIGH LEVEL WALKS
  DOLOMITES
CENTRAL APENNINES OF ITALY

WALKING CENTRAL ITALIAN ALPS
WALKING IN THE DOLOMITES
SHORTER WALKS IN THE DOLOMITES
WALKING ITALY'S GRAN PARADISO
LONG DISTANCE WALKS IN ITALY'S
  GRAN PARADISO
ITALIAN ROCK
WALKS IN THE JULIAN ALPS
WALKING IN SICILY
WALKING IN TUSCANY
VIA FERRATA SCRAMBLES IN THE
  DOLOMITES

OTHER MEDITERRANEAN COUNTRIES
THE ATLAS MOUNTAINS
WALKING IN CYPRUS
CRETE - THE WHITE MOUNTAINS
THE MOUNTAINS OF GREECE
JORDAN - Walks, Treks, Caves etc.
THE MOUNTAINS OF TURKEY
TREKS & CLIMBS WADI RUM JORDAN
CLIMBS & TREKS IN THE ALA DAG
WALKING IN PALESTINE

HIMALAYA
ADVENTURE TREKS IN NEPAL
ANNAPURNA - A TREKKER'S GUIDE
EVEREST - A TREKKERS' GUIDE
GARHWAL & KUMAON - A Trekker's
  Guide
KANGCHENJUNGA - A Trekker's Guide
LANGTANG, GOSAINKUND &
  HELAMBU Trekkers Guide
MANASLU - A trekker's guide

OTHER COUNTRIES
MOUNTAIN WALKING IN AFRICA -
  KENYA
OZ ROCK – AUSTRALIAN CRAGS
WALKING IN BRITISH COLUMBIA
TREKKING IN THE CAUCAUSUS
GRAND CANYON & AMERICAN
  SOUTH WEST
ROCK CLIMBS IN HONG KONG
ADVENTURE TREKS WEST NORTH
  AMERICA
CLASSIC TRAMPS IN NEW ZEALAND

TECHNIQUES AND EDUCATION
SNOW & ICE TECHNIQUES
ROPE TECHNIQUES
THE BOOK OF THE BIVVY
THE HILLWALKER'S MANUAL
THE TREKKER'S HANDBOOK
THE ADVENTURE ALTERNATIVE
BEYOND ADVENTURE
FAR HORIZONS - ADVENTURE
  TRAVEL FOR ALL
MOUNTAIN WEATHER

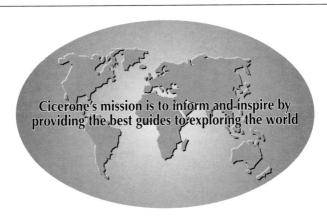

Cicerone's mission is to inform and inspire by providing the best guides to exploring the world

Since its foundation over 30 years ago, Cicerone has specialised in publishing guidebooks and has built a reputation for quality and reliability. It now publishes nearly 300 guides to the major destinations for outdoor enthusiasts, including Europe, UK and the rest of the world.

Written by leading and committed specialists, Cicerone guides are recognised as the most authoritative. They are full of information, maps and illustrations so that the user can plan and complete a successful and safe trip or expedition – be it a long face climb, a walk over Lakeland fells, an alpine traverse, a Himalayan trek or a ramble in the countryside.

With a thorough introduction to assist planning, clear diagrams, maps and colour photographs to illustrate the terrain and route, and accurate and detailed text, Cicerone guides are designed for ease of use and access to the information.

If the facts on the ground change, or there is any aspect of a guide that you think we can improve, we are always delighted to hear from you.

Cicerone Press
2 Police Square Milnthorpe Cumbria LA7 7PY
Tel:01539 562 069   Fax:01539 563 417
e-mail:info@cicerone.co.uk   web:www.cicerone.co.uk